MANAGING THE SOCIAL AND EMOTIONAL NEEDS OF THE GIFTED

A Teacher's Survival Guide

MANAGING THE SOCIAL AND EMOTIONAL NEEDS OF THE GIFTED

A Teacher's Survival Guide

CONNIE C. SCHMITZ

AND JUDY GALBRAITH

(Author of THE GIFTED KIDS SURVIVAL GUIDES)

free spirit
PUBLISHiNG®

Works
for kids™

Library of Congress Cataloging-in-Publication Data

Schmitz, Connie C., 1950-
  Managing the social and emotional needs of the gifted.

  Bibliography: p.
  Includes index.
  1. Gifted children—Education.   2. Gifted children—
Psychology.   3. Teacher-participation in personnel
service.   I. Galbraith, Judy.   II Title.
LC3993.2.S35   1985   371.95   85-80633
ISBN 0-915793-05-9 (pbk.)

Cover and book design by Nancy MacLean
Production art and keyline by Mike Tuminelly
Illustrations by Pete Wagner
20 19 18 17 16 15 14 13 12

Free Spirit Publishing Inc.
400 First Avenue North
Suite 616
Minneapolis, MN 55401

Excerpt from *Frames Of Mind*, page 70, by Howard Gardner, Copyright © 1983 by Howard Gardner. Reprinted by permission of Basic Books, Inc., Publishers.

CONTENTS

It's so hard for me to just be me.
Everyone expects so much of me. I
mean, what's the purpose of life, anyway?

Anonymous, 13-year-old

INTRODUCTION

Not all bright kids have emotional problems, and when they do, these problems may resemble those to which all preteens and adolescents are prone. But researchers, children, parents, and teachers alike are beginning to realize that gifted and talented kids may have special needs that come with being bright. Their view of the world, view of themselves, and other qualities (such as perfectionism and sensitivity) set them apart from peers and family—and at odds with their school—just at a time when desire for conformity is greatest. Only in the last ten years have we begun to address the cognitive needs of our brightest students seriously. To keep them in school and help them mature emotionally as well as intellectually, we must address their affective needs as well.

This book is about understanding, living with, and supporting the social and emotional needs of gifted youth.

Our aims are to:

★ **Increase your sensitivity for students' common issues, problems, and feelings (as perceived and expressed by kids themselves)**

★ **Support your efforts as a gifted ed teacher ... we discuss the problems of working alone in a new field still in the process of defining itself ... we give you some "tough answers" to some of the "tough questions" you'll have to face**

★ **Provide you with concrete strategies for managing students' emotional and social needs**

The goals of these strategies are to help students:

★ **Understand what gifted means, and the purpose of their gifted program**

★ **Resolve conflicts with peers, family, and school personnel**

★ **Take more responsibility for their learning and for their actions**

★ **Understand and accept themselves**

★ **Understand and accept others**

We wrote this book with the classroom teacher foremost in mind—and by this we mean any classroom teacher who works with gifted or talented students, whether in a pull-out or integrated classroom. Our primary audience is the teacher who is relatively new to gifted ed, although veteran teachers should find the current updates and 30 detailed strategies valuable as well. Much of the text would also be useful for school counselors, social workers, psychologists, and gifted education coordinators.

Where This Book "Comes From"

The conflicts and feelings about being gifted have been explored first-hand in hundreds of interviews with elementary and secondary students by Judy Galbraith. As a result of these interviews Judy wrote *The Gifted Kids Survival Guide (For Ages 11-18)* and its successor, *The Gifted Kids Survival*

Guide (For Ages 10 and under). These books talk to gifted students about their mutual concerns: The meaning of giftedness; school conflicts; relationships with parents, teachers, and friends; the pressures to perform. The "eight great gripes of gifted kids," based on these interviews, are clues to the emotional well-being of gifted students—to the conflicts which come "from within and from without."

Many teachers found *The Gifted Kids Survival Guides* useful. In fact, although they were written primarily for students, these books were used by teachers to develop discussion questions and other activities. Due to this response and a growing number of requests, we have expanded upon the original material to produce the guide you see here now.

As authors we are combining several different perspectives and many years of experience in education to fashion this guide. Judy Galbraith (author, educator, publisher), has been teaching gifted students for over nine years. She lectures extensively to teachers, parents, and students on the emotional needs of gifted students. Currently, she is a freelance teacher for several school districts in Minnesota, and is publishing a series of titles in gifted education. Connie Schmitz is a professional freelance writer, working as a research fellow in curriculum and instruction in higher education at the University of Minnesota. Together, we hope to integrate experience, observation, and research to better understand the dimensions of being gifted and to recommend teaching strategies that work.

Several other people have graciously assisted us in this effort. We would like to thank them for doing so. Our thanks to Maureen Mashek, coordinator of the gifted program at South High in Minneapolis, for allowing us to observe several classrooms in her program. Additionally, we are grateful to Lauri Tyson at Susan B. Anthony Junior High (also in Minneapolis) for sharing her students with us. We are particularly indebted to gifted ed teachers Joanne Murray, Joyce

Kennedy, Diane Heacox, and Sue Feigal-Hitch, who spent several hours discussing their teaching and coordinating experiences with us; many of their personal observations appear in these pages. We would like to thank Dr. Tom Greenspon, psychologist, for his thoughts on counseling gifted children and their families. And finally, we appreciate the thoughtful critiques offered by our readers Dee Ames, supervisor of gifted and talented education in Osseo, Minnesota, and Joel Anderson, pro-active counselor and advocate for the gifted in St. Louis Park, Minnesota.

We feel that you, the teacher and educational professional, are working in a very exciting, challenging, but young field of endeavor: nurturing the hearts and minds of exceptional young people. This is not an easy job. We hope this book makes that job a little bit easier.

Connie C. Schmitz and Judy Galbraith

THERE ARE NO LIFE PRESERVERS IN GIFTED ED

Picture the following scene: a special class of young teenagers in a large urban public school.

First there is Gregory, with his lank hair falling in front of his eyes, who is sitting on the edge of his seat. His foot taps the floor in a nonstop staccato rhythm. His eyes are shining; he is busy explaining the proof he wrote on the board for an advanced calculus class. Several people are talking at once. Most audible is Janine, who is loudly groaning for help.

"Ms. Petroff, I'm totally lost—if you want to know why we're not asking questions, it's because we don't know enough to ask questions." Another student goes to the board, demonstrating her method for solving last night's homework. Does Janine get this? "Heck no! I'm drowning! Send in a life preserver!"

A young boy with braces and thin arms, well under five feet tall, confers with his next-door neighbor—a muscular giant whose face is in full hormonal flower. The small boy grins wickedly as he whispers, "I actually did number 21! I'm so proud! As a matter of fact, I have this *incredible* desire to write it on the board."

"Well, go for it!" his friend replies, tossing a crumpled ball of paper in the corner wastepaper basket.

Across the room, various conversations overlap as students review their answers, question the teacher and each other vigorously, and recalculate their figures. "You call that a life preserver?!" Janine says to Gregory, whose proof has still left her in the dark. "Try saying that in English," another kid suggests. (Gregory is a foreign student but obviously well-spoken.) "Who sees this now?" the teacher asks, as she demonstrates a critical step in notation on the board. Silence lasts but a second.

"Hey! That's slick! That's so slick I'm going to write it down!"

"I'm gonna write home about it!"

"I'd say there's a REAL LACK OF LIFE PRESERVERS here! They all have holes in them!"

The three-ring circus begins again, with kids teaching other kids, kids working at the board, the teacher questioning students, checking for comprehension. Students appear to be capable of attending each of the "three rings" simultaneously, for they integrate all the information without much trouble and move on. Their questions are answered once, they understand, and want more.

All eyes go back to the teacher as she writes a new problem on the board. She says very little about it, mentioning only which theorems might come into play. Once the problem is posed, students pounce on it like lions on raw meat. Immediately arguments and questions break out. Just when they seemed to reach an impasse, Janine asks—and then answers—her own question (the teacher silences Gregory in time with a "Sh, Gregory, let's see if she can figure it out"). Janine does get the right answer and the class applauds her with the "high fives" hand slap for which athletes are famous.

When the class is over we ask the teacher to talk about her students: Gregory, who (as the youngest of the class) seems so obviously precocious, and Janine, who struggles dramatically to keep up with the group. The teacher responds that Gregory certainly is bright—he already knows all the material she hopes to cover in the coming year and is enrolled in her university math class. But Janine—Janine is probably the next brightest student in the room.

This example comes from but one class in the country for gifted and talented students. It was an exceptional class in all respects; students were intelligent,

highly motivated, well-behaved, gregarious, and supportive to one another. The teacher was impressive both in
terms of math knowledge and pedagogy; she knew how
to teach bright students, knew how to let them teach
each other, knew how to guide and support their learning
as well as how to stimulate them. Yet even within this
small, homogeneous, well-defined and apparently well-
adjusted group of kids, interesting differences in ability
and affect could be seen.

Gifted Students Are More Different From Each Other Than Alike

This, of course, comes as no surprise. As we'll say
several times throughout the book, there is no one
portrait of a gifted student. Talents and strengths among
the gifted vary as widely as they do with any sample of
students drawn from a so-called average population.
Gregory's obvious facility with terms, computation, and
problem-solving enable him to perform years ahead of his
chronological peers. Janine's math intelligence, on the
other hand, may have been the product of intuition,
originality, or intense interest. Some educators distin-
guish between academically gifted and socially gifted;
between highly gifted, and normally gifted; and between
highly creative and highly talented students. Many other
breakdowns and categories exist.

Neither do all exceptional children share common
psychological traits or personalities; certainly they
express their needs in different ways. Some are outgoing
risk-takers, challengers of the status quo. Some are quiet,
satisfied with their private world. As learners there are
some, like Janine, who need constant feedback. (Fortunately, she was not reluctant to ask for it.) Others need a
tremendous amount of encouragement to perform, or a
lot of structure. Some students interact very little. (One
student read *To Kill A Mockingbird* during the entire
math class we observed.) Others ask for help after class,
or look up a special teacher years later to get advice. And
certainly there are those like Gregory, who appear in

ecstasy, and smile as they radiate intense concentration. ("This is easy!" he remarked.) "Most of these kids demand to be taught," the math teacher said. "Their meters are ticking all the time."

Gifted Programs Also Differ

In addition to diverse talents and emotional profiles among gifted students, there is an equally perplexing variety of gifted ed programs. There are probably as many different types of gifted education classes, programs, and schools as there are teachers and administrators. Although in previous generations "geniuses" were often taken out of the mainstream and allowed to work with special mentors, planned or formal education of exceptional students is a relatively young concept. Those of us who work in gifted programs are on the leading edge of knowledge and the front lines of battle—all at the same time.

Gifted programs vary widely in terms of length, duration, focus, student identification procedures, teacher qualifications, and quality. Researchers working on the Sid W. Richardson study, a survey of 400 schools with gifted ed programs, found that:

> **Nationally the efforts to improve education (for the gifted) are fragmented and discontinuous. Even locally, in schools or districts, programming efforts are likely to be patchwork. Symptomatic is the part-time special class, the "pullout" program, which is the most prevalent practice for educating able learners.[1]**

Basically, secondary and elementary schools are responding to the needs of gifted students in the following ways:

Program Options

Resource areas: A resource room is provided, or special work situations with advanced learning materials, self-study tasks, computer equipment, and so on.

Scheduling: Certain classes are scheduled back to back so students can tackle longer projects or simply cover more material faster.

College courses: High school students take university-level courses or graduate early.

Acceleration: Students move up in a particular subject area or an entire grade level (or two or three).

Enrichment: Special classes are developed to extend or replace regular school curriculum. Enrichment classes typically focus on higher level cognitive skills, such as divergent and evaluative thinking, problem solving, and creativity, (e.g., Olympics of the Mind). Debates, special research projects, courtroom trials, and other experiential learning activities exemplify enrichment classes.

Pull-out: Kids are removed from their regular classrooms for a specified number of hours each week. During these hours, students take special enrichment, accelerated, or other classes or options.

Full-time curriculum: Entirely separate programs for gifted students are developed at specified grade levels. Kids in the program participate for one or more sequential years.

Mentorship programs: Students are paired with professionals in a particular field, be it art, business, research, agriculture, or community affairs.

Independent study: This option can be offered to many students with strong interests who enjoy long-term involvement with projects.

Schools sometimes use one approach but more often they combine programming alternatives. What individual schools are prepared to offer varies widely, depending upon state and local support. Currently, state education agencies, along with other local funds and private grants, provide most of the funding for these programs. Only about 15 percent of the programs responding to the Richardson Study cited federal monies.[1]

Children can be identified for program options in a variety of ways. Often these identification procedures reflect underlying attitudes about giftedness and its definitions. All identification procedures have some problems. For instance, in programs that identify students annually by achievement tests, a child may be gifted in third grade but not in seventh. (Try explaining that to a kid!) Similarly, a student may be gifted in Minnesota but not in Kansas, if state selection criteria stress different types of intelligence. She may even be gifted in one district but not in another, if staff have uneven levels of training and programs are at different stages of development.

Teacher nomination is the most-frequently used means of identifying students according to the Richardson study (92 percent of the respondents used it). Studies by Jacobs[2] and others, however, show teachers to be less accurate in identifying gifted students than parents and peers. In one study in Michigan, teachers were unable to correctly identify any of the 19 students who scored over 135 in IQ tests, even after 6 months of observation. The second-most-used identification measure is standard achievement tests (used by 90 percent of the programs). Unfortunately, research consistently finds no correlation between grades (and IQ scores) and life achievement or success. The Stanford-Binet IQ test is quite reliable for measuring certain types of intelligence and is used approximately 82 percent of the time.[1] But many arguments exist for defining giftedness in broader terms to include creativity and other abilities less easily measured.

Meanwhile, on one end of the spectrum there are programs with comprehensive identification procedures and well-targeted instruction, and on the other end, those with less precise entrance requirements and a "shotgun" approach to instruction. Some students benefit from multiple approaches, receive good career counseling, attend special summer programs, and even spend an entire year (or years) in separate grades. But many get as little as one hour a week of special instruction. Some teachers are brought in to teach classes with no additional training in gifted ed. Others earn masters degrees which encompass specific curriculum areas, process skills, growth and development, and affective needs.

Different Attitudes About Gifted Ed Exist

Attitudes toward gifted students and gifted education vary too. No matter where we look, or who we talk to, we find that "gifted" is a controversial label.

Galbraith's interviews with gifted children under 10 showed that one of the biggest problems was not knowing what gifted meant. They said neither parents nor teachers talk about it. Many kids concluded that it was something secretive and therefore bad, which increased their fears of being different. We suspect virtually all highly gifted kids know they are different by the time they are five or six years old. This awareness of difference can turn into feelings of being strange or weird if the differences are not acknowledged.

> *Well, I tried making him be normal and it just didn't work. I'd say, "Okay, Brian, go out and play," and he'd go on the porch and read music. Or I'd say, "Why don't you invite a friend over?" and he'd invite someone over to play violin duets. So I finally thought, I'm telling him it's wrong to be who he is.*[3]
> *–Mother,*
> *Mpls./St. Paul Magazine, 1985*

Meanwhile, because schools worry about the kids who aren't labeled gifted, they try to minimize the potential for bad feelings by calling their programs "Quest," or "Explorer Clubs." Instead of gifted students these schools have "high flyers" or "high potentials." (By selecting other euphemisms, these schools may feel they're protecting gifted students from the label's stigma, or preventing them from developing "swelled heads." Both can be outcomes of real concern.) Other schools take a deliberate stance on this issue by opening up gifted classes to all students capable of maintaining a B average; these students have the less threatening label "bright" or "high achievers," rather than gifted. Still other schools straightforwardly identify and christen a small population in kindergarten or first grade, stand behind their identification procedures, and track students separately through high school.

As teachers, we've all met some overeager parents who lobby to get their children into the school's gifted program. Then in contrast, there are also those who feel unsettled by their kid's gifted status and would rather keep it quiet. Some children have refused to join a gifted program because they don't want the stigma, or the threat of heavy, new expectations. Some parents occasionally say, "I just wish my child was normal." (Is bright abnormal?)

What these wide discrepancies in attitude and behavior point to are the conflicts which come with thinking about a perhaps inately threatening concept: superior ability. Perhaps these conflicts arise because society is too quick to jump to the conclusion that superior intelligence, talent, or ability means superior people, which implies the rest of humanity is inferior. As a democratic society we are still coming to terms with unequal distribution of "gifts," "unfair" loadings of potential. "If 'superior' people get 'special' attention, isn't that giving them unfair advantage?" the critics ask. Doesn't the existence of gifted ed acknowledge that individual students do not have equal chances to get a piece of the American pie?

As an educational community we are still very much in the process of defining giftedness, of measuring it, and of accepting the gifted student as a legitimate target for instruction. Part of the challenge of gifted ed stems from working in an immature discipline still busy discovering its necessary "truths" and appropriate methods of practice. As Neil Daniel, editor of the *Gifted Students Institute Quarterly*, puts it, "The simple truth is . . . we don't know what intelligence is. We are unable to define giftedness. And we can't say, really, how anybody thinks."[4] This makes advocating gifted ed even more controversial, although no less important. As one of our teacher discussants said,

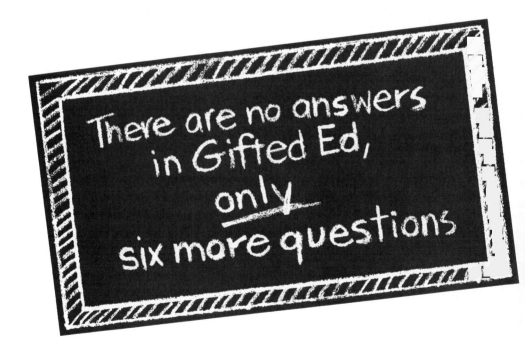

There are no answers in Gifted Ed, only six more questions

Meanwhile, the Gregorys and Janines keep turning up in our classrooms, their eyes sparkling with eagerness and challenge, their worries pouring out—or perhaps locking up within. And highly gifted but underachieving students continue to drop out of school. In some very tragic instances, our brightest young adults commit suicide. These students have a right to education designed for their level of ability. They do not find their way on their own. As educators, we have discriminated against this population in the past for lack of knowledge, and perhaps lack of compassion.

We believe that teachers are going to have to deal with the emotional lives of their students, not just their intellectual needs. In fact, working with students' affective needs may be (in the words of one teacher) "the best thing we can do for them." In an average busy day, with a tight schedule and loaded curriculum, it seems difficult to depart from the teacher's guide to deal with feelings. But as many people have pointed out, if students don't have good self-concepts and good interpersonal relationships, everything else comes to a screeching halt. Affective education belongs in the teacher's guide. And that's what this book is.

Notes

1. June Cox, Neil Daniel, and Bruce Boston, "Executive Summary," *Educating Able Learners: Programs and Promising Practices* (University of Texas Press, 1985).

2. Randy Sue Coburn, "Schooling the Precocious," *Science* (September, 1983):69.

3. Steven Kaplan, "Junior Achievers," *Mpls./St. Paul Magazine* (June, 1985):57.

4. Neil Daniel, "New Questions About Talented People," *Gifted Students Institute Quarterly,* Volume X, No. 15 (1985).

2

ASSESSING WHO YOU'VE GOT: THE GIFTED STUDENT

"Even though we are 'gifted' we still are human. We can make mistakes. No matter how smart we are supposed to be, inside we are just like everyone else."

–Matt, 12

"I used to (more than now) not only have a problem surviving but also thriving and being liked and being 'one of the guys.'"

–Jan, 13

"All my life I've been considered weird or strange."

–Anonymous, 11

"I'm more creative and, well, just different. I don't want to look like Madonna and I think Billy Idol and Van Halen are jerks. Also, I pretend a lot. Bet you didn't know my real name was Theodora Justice! Also, I write BOOKS (yes folks, she did not say *read,* she said *write*). If there's one thing I could change about myself it would be my ribs. They stick out too much. Also I'm such a smart ass. I make myself sick, but I can't help it!"

–Jessie, 12

The Emotional Dimensions of Being Gifted

How gifted kids feel on an emotional level doesn't always match logically with their intellectual capabilities. Brighter does not necessarily mean happier, healthier, more successful, socially adept, or more secure. Neither does brighter necessarily mean hyper, difficult, overly sensitive, or neurotic. In terms of emotional and social characteristics, brighter may not mean anything "different" at all. But while gifted kids do not have a common collection of personality traits, "they do have a common collection of problems."[1]

Like members in any minority, gifted students may feel insecure just because they are different from the norm. Teenagers and preteens in particular want desperately to be like everyone else and any difference, whether positive or negative, is cause for anxiety. But sometimes gifted kids *are* very different; they may feel isolated, alienated, or "weird" as a result. "They have so many problems connecting with other people," teachers have said, "there's a sense of isolation that gets bigger and bigger as years go by, unless some interventions are made." In summarizing Torrance's work with highly creative students, Diane Brode adds, "The nonconforming nature of the highly creative individual is in direct conflict with the extreme conformity demanded by adolescents in groups."[2]

In general, the educational community has been quick to dismiss the emotional problems of high-achieving students for many of the same reasons we have dismissed their intellectual needs. Perhaps we have too many other kids "with worse problems." Perhaps we think "smart kids don't need our help—they've got so much going for them already they should be able to figure it out." Many of us may not realize our brighter students are, in fact, in quite a bit of trouble. They don't necessarily look needy; they seem to have it all together. Used to conquering intellectual problems logically, students themselves may deny their emotional problems by saying, "I'm supposed to be smart. I should be able to think my way out of this." Or, because they are smart, they can successfully delude themselves or rationalize some behavior. Finally, many of us may realize that gifted students suffer emotionally, but aren't sure how to handle it.

Challenges From Within and From Without

Evidence is beginning to accumulate that certain challenges to emotional balance may come automatically with exceptional intellectual ability or talent. Challenges may come both from within the person and from without. Challenges from within include being, by nature, highly perceptive, highly involved, super-sensitive, and perfectionistic. Challenges from without come from conflict with the environment; they surface in the "great gripes" kids have about school or parents or friends.

Extra Perception. Consider, for instance, just the effect that being highly perceptive to stimuli (to sounds, sights, movements, words, patterns, numbers, physical phenomena, or people) would make in one's daily life. Whereas other people might agree, "these two colors match," the artist says, "no, they don't." The musician hears the difference between a note played perfectly and one played slightly off-key. Howard Gardner speaks of the poet as someone who is "superlatively sensitive to the shades of meanings . . . to the sound of words and order of words."[3] Whether their medium is one of language, art, social action, or physics, gifted persons are profoundly sensitive to small differences—and these differences make all the difference.

High Involvement. Sensitivity may breed a certain irritation with the "unsensitive," and unusual preoccupation with interests, tasks, materials, and questions. Whereas other children seem comfortable letting thoughts come and go and relatively unconcerned with unsolved problems and inexact answers, gifted students dream repetitively of treasured problems, pictures, patterns, or concerns. They are obsessed with the intricacy or beauty of phenomena at hand. The creative composer constantly hears tones in his head. The mathematician dreams of proofs; the writer carries precious fragments of verse in his memory. They perceive greater levels of complexity in the world about them, and find this complexity interesting and meaningful.

Super-Sensitivity. In addition to being exquisitely perceptive of and receptive to stimuli, sensitivity in the gifted can also mean moral or emotional sensitivity. Many gifted students are super-sensitive to ethical issues and concerns that are considered unimportant by their peers. As James Alvino comments, they may display "high standards of truth and morality . . . and are quick to judge those who don't measure up. They're affronted by hypocrisy, double standards, and other forms of logical and ethical contradiction."[4] Diane Brode[2] feels they simply mature faster—are morally developed before their peers. Other observers, however, are quick to point out that intellectually precocious children are *not* always emotionally mature for their age; in many cases kids are both emotionally immature and intellectually advanced at the same time.

Perfectionism. Whether this term fits in a pejorative sense or not, gifted people do seem concerned about accomplishment and the pursuit of excellence. This concern is probably rooted, first, in the awareness of quality;

the gifted person is able to discern the difference between the mediocre and superior. Once a person can perceive excellence, can sense "how it ought to be done" (ought to sound, ought to look), she may naturally want to see it done that way. The student who knows quality (or is used to success) may be driven crazy trying to achieve it, simply because he knows what it is, and is quick to sense failure if he cannot. This is why the gifted student needs support to persist despite constant awareness of "failure."

Second, many of the problems students have with high expectations are undoubtedly reinforced by the environment, particularly by their early successes and the commotion this causes. As one ex-"Quiz Kid," Ruth Duskin Feldman, observes; "Whatever I accomplished, it never seemed enough. I had the nagging feeling I should be up there at the top, as I had been in my youth." She also speaks of intelligence as a trap; when children (like the Quiz Kids) are

> . . . accustomed to easy success and . . . are praised for work requiring modest effort [they] may not develop discrimination or learn to meet a challenge. When these children grow up, they seek applause constantly without knowing how to get it. Children held to impossibly high standards and deprived of praise may get caught in a cycle of hopeless, misdirected perfectionism, trying to please parents, teachers, or bosses who never can be satisfied.[5]

Uneven Integration. Challenges to emotional peace can also come from within when a student's intellectual abilities are out of sync. For example, a student who has strong conceptual and verbal skills but a reading disability may feel quite frustrated. Someone with strong spatial ability but weak drawing skills is likely to be similarly stymied. A person may be gifted in bodily-kinesthetic intelligence, but too shy to compete in team sports. Within each of us, certain abilities may or may not combine gracefully or productively.

Although in the past we've tended to stereotype gifted students as exceptional "across the board," few are actually good in everything they do. This type of integrated ability is both rare and exciting. More typical is the student with demonstrated ability in one academic area, or who can transfer one process skill into a number of different content areas. This same student may be a lousy speller, lazy in math, have terrible handwriting, or poor study skills.

We are also becoming more aware of the challenges of emotional well-being that come from "without"—that come from an individual's conflict with the family, school environment, peers, or society in general. These are the gifted students' common problems—the "eight great gripes" identified through interviews with gifted and talented kids and described in *The Gifted Kids Survival Guides:*

These are some of the challenges that come from within and from without for the gifted student. Not all students, of course, suffer all the problems listed above. Some have few adjustment problems generally and feel fine about life. Others experience difficulty in four or five areas. A student's needs will depend on his or her maturity level, type of intelligence, environment, and a whole host of other personality characteristics.

Categories of Gifted Students and Their Needs

With gifted kids so unique, is it possible to generalize about their emotional needs? The answer is yes—with caution, but yes. We can make some generalizations about who is gifted and what their affective needs may be. Moreover, as practitioners, you'll *have* to make some generalizations even though research has yet to substantiate the bigger picture.

This is where knowing your school's selection process will help: just what kind of gifted students are you working with? Students with high verbal or math skills? Kids who score in the exceptionally gifted range on the Stanford-Binet IQ test (150-180)? Kids whose abilities tend to require enrichment opportunities as opposed to accelerated opportunities (or vice versa)? The types of cognitive strengths your students demonstrate may determine, to some extent, the kind of emotional needs they'll have. Keep in mind, however, that our foremost concern should be for what young people say they need help with. Don't deny a kid a reaction, an emotion, or help because she doesn't fit the right category.

There are several frameworks for categorizing students which seem useful to us for predicting their emotional needs. The first has simply to do with the degree of intelligence and the type of intelligence involved.

The *Quantity* and *Quality* of Giftedness Makes a Difference

The degree of difference between the gifted and average student (whether in IQ score, music, language, or chess playing) influences, by itself, the gifted student's self-perception. The young adolescent with a very high IQ (above 150) is likely to feel more different and isolated than kids with IQ scores of 130—simply because he or she is that much more different from the norm. Both are gifted, but because the number of kids in the top 1 to 2 percent of the population is so small, these students are dramatically limited in terms of peer group.

In addition to quantity or degree of ability, giftedness has obvious qualitative differences. Creativity in the visual arts is different than logical-mathematical ability. The interpersonal skills of leadership are different than the linguistic skills of a poet. These areas are equally important; the term "qualitative" suggests intrinsic properties that are unique and special.

Some very exciting work in this area is being done by Howard Gardner,[3] a researcher in education and psychology whose theories on multiple intelligences combine evidence from neurobiology, child development, cognitive psychology, cultural anthropology, and his own studies of idiot savants, brain-damaged adults, and gifted prodigies. Gardner challenges the classical view of intelligence as a construct of single dimension (one is either smart, dumb, or somewhere in between), or dual dimension (one can be talented either in thinking or in feeling). Instead, Gardner suggests there are seven relatively autonomous intelligences which can operate fairly independently, but can also be fashioned and combined in an infinite number of ways.

These seven intelligences are: linguistic, musical, logical-mathematical, spatial, bodily-kinesthetic, interpersonal, and intrapersonal. Gardner is studying how these abilities operate in relative isolation (as with brain-damaged adults, prodigies, and primitive cultures), and how they can be measured and nurtured. Gardner's theories do much to further our understanding of the qualitative differences in intelligence. Profound differences do exist between these abilities: it's not just a simple change in medium. Moreover, abilities characteristically emerge at different ages in human beings (compare the youthful age at which musical prodigies emerge with the mature age at which architects and authors peak). Intelligences can occur in innumerable combinations and strengths, although some pairing is characteristic (musical and mathematical genius together are not uncommon). And finally, the educational strategies which nurture various intelligences most successfully are quite diverse.

Gardner does not discuss how emotional needs may vary with the different intelligences, although he speaks most convincingly of the need to have inter- and intrapersonal intelligence (see Chapter 4). Some teachers say, however, that the math and science-technology students they've known seem to suffer most in terms of isolation. They speculate this is because their vocabulary becomes so highly specialized, the depth of their content knowledge so great, most people can't keep up. Other teachers observe that the kids with integrated abilities—talent spread across a variety of subject areas—seem to have an easier time with life. Students who can't communicate well verbally have the greatest difficulties finding friends.

Accelerated/Enriched Learners

In Colangelo and Zaffran's view,[6] the terms accelerated and enrichment actually "describe qualitatively different needs and learning styles of gifted youngsters and not simply methods of how to provide for those needs."

Accelerated. Accelerated gifted students are interested in mastering and integrating increasingly complex material. They have the ability to learn and recall large amounts of information fast. They are highly efficient information-processors. This type of student craves new information, harder problems; the students' sense of fulfillment comes from mastering higher and higher levels of material and applying it to solve problems of increasing difficulty.

Images of the math student solving a difficult problem comes to mind. The historian who remembers and interprets long, complex sequences of events; the poet or writer who quotes passages verbatim with ease; the doctor who generates four hypotheses and cites 10 particular cases bearing on her diagnosis—these are adult examples of individuals who process, retain, and apply large quantities of knowledge well.

Often, adolescents and pre-adolescents with this type of ability simply "do well" in school. They are high achievers in a well-defined discipline such as science or literature, and succeed in curricular systems which stress knowledge acquisition, linear skill building, and logical analysis. They may also be wholly indifferent to academic subject areas, but suddenly know "everything there is to know" about the Civil War, Reggie Jackson, or the *Lord of the Rings Trilogy*.

Enriched. The enriched gifted student, in contrast, has the ability to become wholly involved or immersed in a problem, to "form a relationship" with a topic. These students focus on the problem—their relation to it and the learning process—as an end in itself, rather than a means to accumulate more knowledge.

Enriched students may also be highly emotional, imaginative, internally motivated, curious, and driven to explore and to experiment. They tend to be reflective and emotionally mature. Frequently, they have a keen sense of humor. The enriched student becomes passionate about a subject, a project, or a cause, often pursuing it with fierce energy.

Artists, musicians, dancers, writers, and actors tend to fall into this category, although research scientists, political activists, religious leaders, lawyers, and educators are other adult examples. The child who writes, directs, and stars in a play is demonstrating "enrichment" characteristics, as is the student who designs and constructs a futuristic model city, students who "live and breathe" dinosaurs, computers, or entrepreneurial businesses. Enriched students thrive on discovery and experience.

In terms of counseling or emotional need, the accelerated learner is most frustrated by lock-step learning. He needs to move on and master more material, not do endless drill and practice. Because these students have high achievement expectations (e.g., score 100 percent on every test), they may need help setting realistic (or at least humane) goals for themselves. Teachers and parents can "overdrive" achievers in this category, which then reinforces the student's fear of failing. This student may also be socially immature compared to his mental peers, and need help learning social skills.

Enriched learners, in contrast, aren't especially concerned with achievement (and may never be the top academic performers in a content area), but they invest a significant amount of emotional energy in what they do. In return, they require teachers who are sensitive to their intense feelings of frustration, passion, enthusiasm, idealism, anger, and despair. Enriched students may also need adult support to persist with a single task, or to harness their energies more efficiently.

Female, Ethnic Minority, and Handicapped Learners

Other categories of giftedness which may predict emotional needs include gifted females, minorities, and handicapped.[7,8] Generally, the needs of these groups are related to being bright and in an underachieving minority at the same time.

Females. Gifted girls continue to face special conflicts in resolving society's expectations of them as women and as gifted people, despite the impact the women's movement made on role definitions during the 1970s. More than ever before, women are deciding to delay or forego childrearing as a full (or part-time) occupation in order to pursue careers. As of this writing a majority of women in the United States hold full time jobs outside the home.

Still, in junior and senior high school, girls are exposed to many deep-seated cultural taboos which make it difficult for them to comfortably display their intelligence and pursue excellence as aggressively as boys. The result of this inhibition can be long-term depression and very low self-esteem.

For gifted girls who do express their abilities, further conflicts can result. Whereas bright students are told to develop their talents and be selfish in the pursuit of their goals, women are expected to be selfless, nurturing, and supportive of others. Gifted students are often active, exploring, and assertive by nature, yet women are supposed to be "sweet, dependent June Allyson types pretending to be overawed by the opposite sex."[6] A gifted female today has more assertive role models than ever before, but women's careers continue to place second to men's in dual-career marriages. They generally earn less income and (when children are involved) are expected to perform most parenting duties. No one asks high school or college age males what they're going to do about day care for their children when they talk about career plans.

For adolescent girls, busy with the work of establishing a sexual identity, sexual confusion may result. The question is how to be feminine and talented at the same time. "When I was 10 years old and entered seventh grade . . . one of the popular girls took me aside and said, 'Don't raise your hand so much, the boys don't like it.' "[5] As adults, gifted and motivated women literally have to consider rejecting part of their sexuality (i.e., conception and childbirth) if they want to achieve in particularly demanding fields such as law or medicine. Meanwhile, gifted girls have to deal with the biases of some school counselors who are slow to identify them as bright, or who counsel them into sex-stereotyped fields.

Minorities. A similar dilemma develops for gifted minority students who have to resolve being black (or Chicano or Native American) and succeeding in a white classroom at the same time. In trying to develop his or her talents or interests, the gifted minority student can get caught between two cultures. To illustrate: in a recent workshop with gifted Native American teenagers, a 15-year-old-boy remarked, "Some of the people in the Indian community think I've sold out because I go to a challenging private school."

Sometimes the conflict stems from peer pressure to resist white authority figures or the white "system" generally. Other times, just being different from one's parents, family, and ethnic community causes guilt or anxiety. Like children of immigrants to this country, gifted minority students may feel conflicted about being more successful in the white majority culture than their parents. The adjustments and other conflicts may be less painful for Asian students, however, for a disproportionately high number of them are gifted, and many learn quite successfully in American school systems.

Sometimes, gifted minority students aren't recognized as talented or able because their gifts lie in areas that are celebrated by their ethnic group but not by Western society generally. For instance, minority gifted are often talented in "imagery, creativity, dance, and humor"[7]—areas which American educators have been slow to recognize as legitimate forms of intelligence and which are difficult to measure. Further, when cognitive skills are assessed via achievement tests and English is not their native language, gifted minorities may test below their ability level and be inappropriately labeled and counseled. "Intelligence" is, as Howard Gardner[3] so eloquently states, a culturally defined and conditioned capability. A society that values navigational skills, for instance, shapes its children from an early age to direct a canoe at night by the stars, and considers its best navigators the wise men of the tribe. The spatial ability required by this feat is less prized in American culture.

Because the abilities we value in human beings are very much tied to the products our society needs or cherishes, we cannot help but define intelligence in terms of cultural priorities and character. The academic traditions in this country mirror Western concepts of intelligence generally: rational thought and the cognitive domain (normally measured by IQ and achievement tests) are the rule and not the exception. Both in conception and in fact, these notions and these instruments impart a cultural bias.

Minority gifted may, of course, be talented in similar areas and in similar ways as majority students. But it comes as no surprise that, in many cases, cultural heritage continues to influence how minority gifted develop and express their talents.

Physical Handicaps/Learning Disabilities. Research finds high-ability individuals in all handicapped areas, but traditional identification procedures remain largely inadequate for these people. As a result, this may indicate a small but highly underserved population.

In thinking of Helen Keller, we're reminded of how difficult it was for her to find people and programs to educate and treat her. We remember her intense struggle to communicate with the world, and her emotional isolation before Annie became her teacher. We also reflect on how extraordinarily gifted she must have been to learn concepts—the whole meaning and flow of language—through the medium of hand signals alone. For those of us with sight and hearing it's difficult to separate our knowledge from our visual and auditory perception of the world: Keller's learning, in contrast, was independent of such experiences, and relied heavily on sensory, linguistic (in the abstract, not vocal, sense), and spatial intelligence.

Three important points concerning gifted handicapped students are made by Colangelo and Zaffran:[7]

1) **Gifted handicapped may be "high in perception and abstraction but can't translate this to performance because of their handicap." Instead, the inability to "perform a task is associated with the inability to think and understand."**

2) **Teachers and adults may automatically lower their expectations for gifted handicapped, who develop even lower self-concepts "because of their situation and the low expectations of others."**

3) **Gifted handicapped are an unseen minority. When teacher and parent groups are asked to imagine a gifted child, they rarely conjure up the image of a handicapped student.**

The emotional needs of female, minority, and handicapped students reflect the isolation and conflict of their respective situations. All of these students need encouragement to be all that they can be despite the risks of leaving a previously defined role or community. They would especially benefit from the presence of more role models, which can be presented in the form of teachers or presenters, graphic displays, verbal examples, biographies, special reports, or projects. When teachers become systematic about including examples of handicapped, culturally diverse, and female gifted role models, they are enabling attitudes and expectations to change.

In summary of our discussion so far, the distinction between enriched and accelerated gifted, and the special tasks of female, minority, and handicapped students are useful clues for assessing student's emotional needs. Another scheme proposed by Barbara Clark[8] analyzes gifted characteristics independent of sex, race, culture, or learning style.

Cognitive and Affective Characteristics

Clark divides gifted characteristics into five categories: Cognitive, affective, physical, intuitive, and societal. The first two categories deserve particular attention. The following two tables summarize what Clark sees as defining characteristics of the gifted, examples of their related needs, and possible subsequent problems.

Differential Cognitive Characteristics	Examples of Related Needs	Possible Concomitant Problems
Extraordinary quantity of information, unusual retentiveness	To be exposed to new and challenging information of the environment and the culture, including aesthetic, economic, political, educational, and social aspects; to acquire early mastery of foundation skills	Boredom with regular curriculum; impatience with "waiting for the group"
Advanced comprehension	Access to challenging curriculum and intellectual peers	Poor interpersonal relationships with less able children of the same age; adults considering children "sassy" or "smart alec"; a dislike for repetition of already understood concepts
Unusually varied interests and curiosity	To be exposed to varied subjects and concerns; to be allowed to pursue individual ideas as far as interest takes them	Difficulty in conforming to group tasks; overextending energy levels, taking on too many projects at one time
High level of language development	To encounter uses for increasingly difficult vocabulary and concepts	Perceived as a "show off" by children of the same age
High level of verbal ability	To share ideas verbally in depth	Dominate discussions with information and questions deemed negative by teachers and fellow students; use of verbalism to avoid difficult thinking tasks

Differential Cognitive Characteristics	Examples of Related Needs	Possible Concomitant Problems
Unusual capacity for processing information	To be exposed to ideas at many levels and in large variety	Resents being interrupted; perceived as too serious; dislike for routine and drill
Accelerated pace of thought processes	To be exposed to ideas at rates appropriate to individual pace of learning	Frustration with inactivity and absence of progress
Flexible thought processes	To be allowed to solve problems in diverse ways	Seen as disruptive and disrespectful to authority and tradition
Comprehensive synthesis	To be allowed a longer incubation time for ideas	Frustration with demands for deadlines and for completion of each level prior to starting new inquiry
Early ability to delay closure	To be allowed to pursue ideas and integrate new ideas without forced closure or products demanded	If products are demanded as proof of learning, will refuse to pursue an otherwise interesting subject or line of inquiry
Heightened capacity for seeing unusual and diverse relationships	To mess around with varieties of materials and ideas	Frustration at being considered "off the subject" or irrelevant in pursuing inquiry in areas other than subject being considered; considered odd or weird by others
Ability to generate ideas and solutions	To build skills in problem solving and productive thinking; opportunity to contribute to solution to meaningful problems	Difficulty with rigid conformity; may be penalized for not following directions; may deal with rejection by becoming rebellious
Early differential patterns for thought processing (e.g., thinking in alternatives, abstract terms, sensing consequences, making generalizations)	To be exposed to alternatives, abstractions, consequences of choices, and opportunities for drawing generalizations and testing them	Rejection or omission of detail; questions generalizations of others, which may be perceived as disrespectful behavior
Early ability to use and form conceptual frameworks	To use and to design conceptual frameworks in information gathering and problem solving; to seek order and consistency; to develop a tolerance for ambiguity	Frustration with inability of others to understand or appreciate original organizations or insights; personally devised systems or structure may conflict with procedures of systems later taught

An evaluative approach to themselves and others	To be exposed to individuals of varying ability and talent, and to varying ways of seeing and solving problems; to set realistic, achievable short-term goals; to develop skills in data evaluation and decision making	Perceived by others as elitist, conceited, superior, too critical; may become discouraged from self-criticism, can inhibit attempting new areas if fear of failure is too great; seen by others as too demanding, compulsive; can affect interpersonal relationships as others fail to live up to standards set by gifted individual; intolerant of stupidity
Persistent, goal-directed behavior	To pursue inquiries beyond allotted time spans, to set and evaluate priorities	Perceived as stubborn, willful, uncooperative

Differential Affective Characteristics	Examples of Related Needs	Possible Concomitant Problems
Large accumulation of information about emotions that has not been brought to awareness	To process cognitively the emotional meaning of experience, to name one's own emotions, to identify one's own and others' perceptual filters and defense systems, to expand and clarify awareness of the physical environment, to clarify awareness of the needs and feelings of others	Information misinterpreted affecting the individual negatively
Unusual sensitivity to the expectations and feelings of others	To learn to clarify the feelings and expectations of others	Unusually vulnerable to criticism of others, high level of need for success and recognition
Keen sense of humor—may be gentle or hostile	To learn how behaviors affect the feelings and behaviors of others	Use of humor for critical attack upon others resulting in damage to interpersonal relationships
Heightened self-awareness, accompanied by feelings of being different	To learn to assert own needs and feelings nondefensively, to share self with others, for self-clarification	Isolate self, resulting in being considered aloof, feeling rejected; perceive difference as a negative attribute resulting in low self-esteem and inhibited growth emotionally and socially
Idealism and sense of justice, which appear at an early age	To transcend negative reactions by finding values to which he or she can be committed	Attempt unrealistic reforms and goals with resulting intense frustration (Suicides result from intense depression over issues of this nature.)

Earlier development of an inner locus of control and satisfaction	To clarify personal priorities among conflicting values To confront and interact with the value system of others	Difficulty conforming; reject external validation and choose to live by personal values that may be seen as a challenge to authority or tradition
Unusual emotional depth and intensity	To find purpose and direction from personal value system To translate commitment into action in daily life	Unusual vulnerability; problem focusing on realistic goals for life's work
High expectations of self and others, often leading to high levels of frustration with self, others, and situations Perfectionism	To learn to set realistic goals and to accept setbacks as part of the learning process To hear others express their growth in acceptance of self	Discouragement and frustration from high levels of self-criticism; problems maintaining good interpersonal relations as others fail to maintain high standards imposed by gifted individuals; immobilization of action due to high levels of frustration resulting from situations that do not meet expectations of excellence
Strong need for consistency between abstract values and personal actions	To find a vocation that provides opportunity for actualization of student's personal value system, as well as an avenue for his or her talents and abilities	Frustration with self and others leading to inhibited actualization of self and interpersonal relationships
Advanced levels of moral judgment	To receive validation for nonaverage morality	Intolerance of and lack of understanding from peer group, leading to rejection and possible isolation

Clark hypothesizes that with each of these characteristics, attendant needs and possible emotional problems can be drawn. For instance, a student who can generate highly original ideas and solutions will probably have difficulty learning in a highly structured, preset curriculum where there is little flexibility, or go berserk with repetitious drill and practice. Someone particularly adept at processing information may dislike interruptions, and be perceived as too serious. A person with unusual emotional depth and intensity may leave himself or herself inappropriately vulnerable or have problems focusing on realistic goals for life's work.

Readers should remember that Clark's framework analyzes characteristics of cognitive and affective gifts, and not gifted people per se. Rarely is someone gifted in the cognitive domain to the total exclusion of the affective, nor are they equally gifted in all cognitive traits. Some highly divergent thinkers may have lousy memories, read poorly, or assimilate information indifferently. Nonetheless, looking at a student's dominant cognitive and affective strengths may help predict which kinds of emotional challenges they'll encounter.

Composite Portraits

We began this chapter by looking at the emotional dimensions of being gifted (challenges from within and without) and several types of gifted students: normally and profoundly gifted, gifted in one of the seven intelligences, accelerated/enriched, female, minority, handicapped, and cognitive/affective. It may be that the type of gifted students you have will determine, to some extent, the kind of emotional problems they'll encounter.

Rarely do students show up in your classroom, however, as perfect models of this category or that classification. For this reason, we'd like to close this section with composite portraits of gifted students offered by Webb, Meckstroth, and Tolan[9] in their excellent book,

Guiding the Gifted Child. In their opening chapter these authors describe what gifted children are like generally, although some kids obviously demonstrate certain traits more than others, and virtually no student manifests the complete range of characteristics. For this reason we summarize their descriptions into the following portraits.

Many gifted children are energetic, enthusiastic, eager to explore ideas and overcome challenges. These students are highly divergent thinkers, viewing the world in nontraditional ways, and (at certain stages) are ready to demonstrate their individuality through nonconforming behavior, dress, or interests.

This kind of student may need to show you that she sees and does things differently. She thrives on asking questions and generating alternatives. Her need to experiment, to test, to push may cause adults to label her as being aggressive, argumentative, or manipulative. (She may also be, in fact, aggressive and manipulative, and her intelligence enables her to be so quite masterfully.)

Another gifted student has very intense but sporadic interests or work habits. He pursues activities compulsively, fanatically, then suddenly shifts his focus to another subject, skill, or person. Adults may view this learning process as disorganized or scattered. A trap which this gifted learner may fall into is setting unrealistically high goals or standards before he has the skills to meet these standards. Then, what objectively is unusual achievement may be interpreted by the child as failure.

Another variation of emotional style is the extraordinarily sensitive student who wonders at the changes of fall foliage, sheds tears of passion upon hearing Beethoven, or becomes absolutely absorbed in fascination with a prism of light. This student may be so emotionally attuned she feels the feelings of other people before they're aware of them. Or, she may sense the implication or relationship of events which other people discount.

And if her ability to perceive problems outstrips her skills for coping, she may become seriously anxious and depressed.

Webb, Meckstroth, and Tolan go on to describe a kind of existential crisis which some exceptionally bright children experience when much of the world around them seems irrational and uncaring. To some kids, the world appears to be in the hands of incompetent adults who accept injustice and incongruity all too easily. These same adults, pedantic or self-serving or both, also expect the gifted "adults of tomorrow" to remedy their toughest problems. Assuming responsibility for this kind of world can be quite overwhelming for a young person.

Other gifted children opt to spend their time both silent and invisible, waiting for others to grow up or catch up to their level. Then, they think, they'll find acceptance and companionship. Meanwhile, they dream of endless ways to fill up "wasted time."

In terms of emotional need, these authors believe that all gifted students need special amounts of acceptance and approval *as people*, particularly if all their self-worth is tied up with accomplishments, performances, or products. A serious dilemma in self-esteem results when students feel other people value them only because they are smart, get good grades, or perform well. Whereas other children are loved simply for being alive, for being funny, cheerful, loyal, companionable, or helpful, gifted kids sometimes wonder if they'll be loved if they stop achieving. Too anxious to test this hypothesis, they channel all their energy into achieving.

Bright students are quick to spot the adult who is riding on their coattails—feeding off their accomplishments because it makes their teaching look good, or validates their parenting. The compliant gifted student who spends an entire childhood pleasing his parents and teachers with grades or performances may find little pleasure in his accomplishments as an adult, no matter how compulsively he strives for them. Students feeling this kind of pressure may need help finding the courage to be average until they achieve a sense of ownership over their successes and their failures.

Like virtually every author we reviewed, Webb, Meckstroth, and Tolan concur with our conclusions that bright children need help understanding their feelings. They need to:

★ Know how they are similar to and different from other people

★ Feel pride in their abilities, rather than guilt or anxiety

★ Learn how to value and accept people less able than themselves

★ Own their own talents and determine how they best fit into the world

★ Belong to a group, and to the school community

Recognizing Emotional and Social Problems

Each year, more than 80,000 students in the top 25 percent of the population intellectually leave school before graduation.[10] Although we don't know what percentage of these students fall into gifted categories, we do know they constitute 11 percent of all dropouts annually, and that they score 110 or above on IQ tests.

Signs of Trouble

Dropping out is only one way gifted students can go awry. As one teacher commented to us about her gifted classes (K-12), "I've always got a kid in trouble." Her examples of trouble included everything from the inability to concentrate to the need for attention, physical closeness, and affection; from poor school work and attendance to disruptions in class and dropping out.

In terms of everyday sorts of dysfunction, unhappy gifted kids display the same patterns and symptoms as other children do. They brag, tease, put others down, avoid responsibility, develop a "negative attitude," confront adults relentlessly, stop working, stop trying, withdraw. A seriously troubled student is one who seems isolated, who stops participating at school and at home, whose disinterest seems to pervade every conceivable subject or occupation. Students trapped in this sort of inertia cause some teachers and parents to feel hopeless themselves: "I'm just not getting through to him, no matter what I try." When we asked teachers (see Teacher Inventory in the Appendix) which types of gifted kids they had the hardest time working with they frequently answered, "the underachievers, the unmotivated, the apathetic, those full of grudges, the snobs, the ones who have 'given up on the system.'"

Frequently, teachers can recognize low self-esteem or depression most clearly in students' body language. The chin-on-chest, a low or inaudibly pitched voice, habitual mumbling, lack of eye contact, and lethargic body posture are all signs of poor self-concept.

Similarly, the student who is demonstrably angry, who loses control easily, underachieves, and has no close friends but plenty of "associates in class crime" is also a troubled kid. A sense of powerlessness and rage came through in the words of one teenage boy we observed during a group discussion about school: "What's the point of confronting teachers on how boring the damn school is? The teachers aren't going to change!" As the boy continued to blast away at "the system" and everything else in sight, we noticed how difficult it was for him to use the pronoun "I." Other people were at fault and other people projected his sentiments. Yet he wasn't able to say what he was feeling—anger? Fear? Frustration? When asked to use the word "I" so the group could recognize who he was talking about and what he was feeling, the student could not (would not) comply. Inability to own feelings and opinions is a sign of emotional conflict and lack of insight.

Symptoms of the seriously depressed or suicidal teenager have been well documented by James DeLisle and others since the very sad death of an extremely bright and seemingly successful teenage boy in Texas. Depressed gifted students may, because of their sensitivity, become "hostages of their own special insights," and need immediate support and help in coping with reality. The three danger signals described by Delisle[11] are:

1. **Self-imposed isolation from family and peers; avoiding all social occasions and invitations.**

2. **Self-imposed perfection as the ultimate standard, to the point that the only tasks enjoyed are the ones completed perfectly. "Striving to succeed" becomes a struggle merely to maintain current levels of performance.**

3. **Deep concern with personal powerlessness to affect adult situations and world events.**

To this list we would also add narcissism (total preoccupation with self and with fantasy), unusual fascination with violence, eating disorders such as bulimia and anorexia, chemical abuse, and any other rigidly compulsive behaviors (even excessive studying and running marathons). Ask yourself, "Have I ever seen this kid relax?" Although it would be inappropriate to approach every gifted student as a potential suicide, teachers should take all talk of death seriously. It should never be brushed aside.

Inventorying Students

Now that we've talked about the emotional dimensions of being talented and bright, the conflicts from within and without, and about specific needs particular categories of students may have, how would you describe your students? What kinds of problems and needs would you say they have?

One way to provide yourself with answers is to assess how students feel about themselves through an inventory we've designed (see Student Inventory in the

Appendix). This survey is for all gifted and talented students. Its purpose is twofold:

1. **It will give you a reading on how your students feel about themselves and others, on what they think being gifted and being in a gifted class means, and how seriously affected they are by problems known to surface among gifted youth.**

2. **It will stimulate kids to think about these conflicts, their areas of strength and need, and their feelings.**

The inventory is a good first strategy for discussing these issues because it is anonymous. As such, the survey won't give you answers from specific individuals (you may know some authors by their answers, nonetheless). It can answer the following questions collectively:

★ **Why do students think they are in your class?**

★ **What do students think the class is all about?**

★ **What do students think gifted (or whatever label is used) means?**

★ **In what ways do students feel different from most other peers?**

★ **In what ways do students feel the same?**

★ **How do students score on the Eight Great Gripes?**

★ **What other emotional problems do students have?**

★ **What do students do to feel good about themselves?**

You may wish to modify the survey in some way for your students. For instance, younger children may need a shortened form and slightly different lists under certain items. Older students may need differently worded instructions. We've found that the more time we spend introducing the survey and our purposes, the better data we receive. High school students in our pilot group took about 15 minutes to complete the survey, junior high students slightly longer. We suggest you *don't* assign the survey as homework (you won't get many questionnaires back), and don't give students only five minutes at the end of the day to complete it. Rather, we recommend using the survey as a learning activity, and giving them time at the beginning of class to fill it out. Administer a form at the beginning and at the end of the program for comparison, or use a variation of it as an evaluation form.

Notes

1. Susan D. Allen and Donna K. Fox, "Group Counseling the Gifted," *Journal for the Education of the Gifted* 3(2):83.

2. Diane S. Brode, "Group Dynamics With Gifted Adolescents," *Gifted/Creative/Talented* (November/December, 1980):61.

3. Howard Gardner, *Frames of Mind: The Theory of Multiple Intelligences* (New York: Basic Books, Inc., 1983).

4. James Alvino, "Guidance for the Gifted," *Instructor* (November/December, 1981):65.

5. Ruth Duskin Feldman, "The Promise and Pain of Growing Up Gifted," *Gifted/Creative/Talented* (May/June, 1985):1.

6. Nicholas Colangelo and Ronald T. Zaffran, "Special Issues in Counseling the Gifted," *Counseling and Human Development* 11(5):2.

7. Nick Colangelo, "Myths and Stereotypes of Gifted Students: Awareness for the Classroom Teacher," in *Multicultural, Nonsexist Education: A Human Relations Approach,* N. Colangelo, C. H. Foxley, and R. Dustin, Eds.

8. Barbara Clark, *Growing Up Gifted, 2nd ed.* (Westerville, Ohio: Charles E. Merrill Publishing Company, 1983). (Dubuque, Iowa: Kendall Hunt Publishing Company, 1979), p. 1.

9. James T. Webb, Elizabeth A. Meckstroth, and Stephanie S. Tolan, *Guiding the Gifted Child* (Columbus, Ohio: Ohio Psychology Publishing Company, 1982), chap. 1.

10. Joseph L. French, "Characteristics of High Ability Dropouts," *National Association of Secondary School Principals (NASSP) Bulletin* (February, 1969):68.

11. James R. Delisle, *Gifted Children Monthly* (February, 1984).

3

ASSESSING WHO YOU ARE: THE GIFTED ED TEACHER

"If I make a mistake, other teachers say, 'And *you* teach the gifted?!' "

"Everyone thinks you have an easy job—the easiest kids (cream-of-the-crop, no need for prep-time, right?)"

"I get asked all sorts of questions just because I teach gifted, such as 'How many eggs do loons lay?' Now why would I have the vaguest idea how many eggs loons lay?"

"This is definitely not a 'cush' job."

–Gifted Ed Teachers, Minnesota

Attitudes About Giftedness

Have you noticed that teachers of the gifted suffer many of the same stereotypes that gifted students themselves do? Somehow, parents, colleagues, and administrators seem to think gifted ed teachers should know all the answers; life for them is probably easier than it is for the rest of us; gifted ed teachers probably think they're better teachers. Like gifted students, gifted ed teachers may also lack supportive peers, either because they are physically the only person in the building (or district!) working in gifted ed, or because they are subtly ostracized. ("No one wants to hear about my problems," a teacher managing 120 gifted kids from 12 grade levels told us.)

Contrary to these misconceptions, teaching gifted students is an extremely demanding job. The kids have tremendous physical and psychic energy, and are "on to you" in a minute—they know when you're unprepared. Yet gifted ed teachers are capable of making mistakes like any other human being. Furthermore, it's not possible to know all the answers when working with little "content experts." By training and experience you may be better prepared to work in certain subject matter areas than with others. But no matter what your training, a tremendous amount of preparation is necessary before each class and few substantial curricular materials exist. ("There's no workbook out there, and whatever you use has got to be good or you're dead!")

As for feeling like gifted ed teachers are "better teachers," the comparison is irrelevant. One hopes we *are* good teachers, that we have chosen to work with the gifted because we feel most successful with or drawn to this group. Similarly, one also hopes that teachers working with other populations would be best for their assignments — any one of us may be real washouts with particular assignments we're not interested in. But here again is an instance where people's attitudes about giftedness show some inner conflict.

Coming to Terms With the Label

That "gifted" is a controversial label you know well enough, probably through personal experience. Think back to your first introduction to the term: what did you think it meant? Think back to your first parent or staff meeting on the proposed gifted ed class or program. (Or even a current one, for that matter!) Remember what people's reactions were?

One mother we know recently had a five-year-old child score above 150 on the Stanford-Binet IQ test. Both she and the school had suspected that the boy was gifted. When she called her relatives to tell them the surprising news their only response was, "Oh, boy, I bet you're going to have trouble with him now." We compared this reaction to telling a friend that you had, for instance, just inherited a million dollars or won a grand prize, and being told, "I bet you'll have to pay a lot of taxes on that load!"

"In general, I don't tell many people," this mother said. "I get the feeling they'd be a whole lot more supportive if I said my son had a learning disability."

As we suggested in Chapter One, the very language people use to describe gifted students indicates how easily they embrace the concept of exceptional intellect or talent. For some reason, it is easier for society to name, praise, and financially reward the outstanding athlete (and the outstanding entertainer) than the brilliant mathematician or poet. The teasing that "brain kids" endure in junior and senior high school contrasts sharply with the celebration that "jocks" enjoy.

To some people, gifted suggests elitism in the racial or class sense, i.e., kids selected for gifted programs are simply well-behaved, upper middle-class, and white. They fear that the inherent cliquishness of ability grouping will invite the "good test-takers" to assume the mantle of moral and intellectual superiority. Both these concerns are probably true in what we fervently hope to be isolated incidences. Whenever gifted programs do drift towards biased selection processes, or infer undue privilege to certain students, they do real damage to the credibility of gifted ed. Nonetheless, it's important to realize that resentments come inevitably with the selection process itself. By identifying one group as gifted, does that make all other children "ungifted"? Aren't we all equal, and all special? Well, yes . . . .

Parents whose children are not selected for the program may question whether gifted students are getting different kinds or levels of instruction, or whether they're simply getting *better* instruction. Wouldn't gifted ed programs benefit the average child, too? They worry that student performance in "regular" classrooms will go down, once the top-level students are pulled out. (The opposite is true; able children may suddenly find themselves blossoming without the presence of clearly advanced students. It's as though the way has been cleared for them to perform.)

Disagreement over the term extends to educational professionals as well. In the previously mentioned Richardson study,[1] authors Cox, Daniel, and Boston promote more generalized labels and resist calling any group of students "the gifted." They recommend that schools broaden their assessment processes by testing all students, and relaxing cut-off scores. They favor "throwing a wide net in early childhood and later allowing the educational programming to select those students with unusual talent and motivation." Other leaders believe that to water down the definition is to lose whatever momentum the movement has gained; the end result would (again) be inadequate education for the children at the highest levels of ability.

Like it or not, the label "gifted" is here today and we need to get used to it. In our view, all labels are equally bad, and calling kids "high flyers" as opposed to "gifted" fools no one, and imparts a sense of secrecy (shame? false modesty?) as well. Intelligence is a good thing. So is athletic ability. We don't go out of our way to call the football team something other than the football team, or athletes anything other than athletes. Why must we call our brightest students something other than bright, or talented? Parents who try to protect their child from the label may end up doing more damage; kids will hear the label anyway, yet have no skills for defusing and processing it.

One teacher commented, "I don't think any of us in the field can give up the term (gifted) because we've finally been able to get it accepted and recognized on a national level." This is an important point, because designing curriculum to serve newly identified needs or populations is definitely a political act. As another teacher said, "Politics is right up there next to direct service. You're constantly involved with politics." And a political movement or group cannot survive without a name.

How students feel about their abilities and the label "gifted" (or whatever group name is used) will depend a great deal on how their parents and teachers feel about them, and how they use the term. Therefore, your attitudes about giftedness are critical.

When we piloted our Teacher Survey on gifted ed teachers we asked them whether or not they use the label "gifted." Here are some of their responses:

"I use it because it is good to get it into the vocabulary and to become used to it. It shouldn't be a word to avoid."

"I try not to use it because it is so misunderstood and misused."

"I haven't felt qualified to use this label."

"A gift is something you've been given and you shouldn't have to apologize for that."

"It is appropriate although it often means different things to each person hearing it."

"I do not use it all the time because of the problems it creates for kids. I do use it in specific sessions to help them know how to deal with the label."

"I use it for lack of anything better but I don't like labeling any student, whether they are slow or advanced. Teachers do need to categorize students but I don't think students need to hear the labels we place on them."

"What's wrong with the word gifted? Everyone knows what it means — Downs Syndrome still means retarded and it will soon become negative for that reason and a nicer word will replace it."

How Do You Feel About Your Own Abilities?

Suppose we were to ask this question: Are you gifted? What would you answer?

If you're reading this book in 1985 or thereabouts, you probably don't know if you are officially "gifted" or not; as an educational descriptor this term wasn't coined until the federal guidelines appeared in 1976.

But suppose you are not gifted—you know your IQ score is below 130, you were an average student and developed no outstanding abilities. You failed to get into an Ivy League college and didn't complete four years of college ahead of your time. Is that bad? Does that make you an inadequate teacher? Does that mean you have nothing to offer, no special qualities? Does that make you a less valuable person? Of course not!

Many important jobs in the world don't require genius-level intelligence, and they may require attributes that other people have in abundance. According to one theory,[2] the optimum range of intelligence runs from 125-145 on the Stanford-Binet IQ test. People who score in this range are able to master most tasks, work in any occupation they choose, and may function more easily in the world than people with profoundly high IQ scores. And let us not forget that high intelligence is also only one set of personal characteristics that we value: loyalty, honesty, humor, joy, and enthusiasm are important, useful virtues.

But suppose you are—or think you may be—in the upper 3 percent of the population in intellectual ability.

Would you stand up in a meeting with school colleagues (everyone from the principal and secretaries to regular teachers, coaches, and luncheon staff) to be identified? Would you want your name in the paper? How would you tell your friends or relatives—or would you? Would telling them help explain what you're all about, or merely intimidate them? Are you comfortable with your abilities, or anxious? If you're ambivalent about it, imagine how confused young students are!

Perhaps, you say, recognition for a job well done is okay, it's just the effect of the term gifted itself, the calling-to-attention of an abstract quality that people can't really define but envy anyway. On the other hand, it may be the "packaging" of your personal abilities you resist. "What am I," you say, "A commodity for others to trade on?!" And then there's your sense of justice (and injustice): perhaps you know plenty of people just as capable as you who don't "get identified." How fair is that? And then perhaps you know plenty of people who have the label—but for the life of you, you can't see why!

These are some common reactions you (or others) may have when thinking about this label. Because most of us haven't lived through this era of ability grouping, we can only guess what it is like to be told in second, fifth, or tenth grade that one's abilities are extraordinary and require special instruction. We do know that it is a label students will live with for the rest of their lives, and if they can't talk about it with their gifted ed teacher, then who *can* they talk about it with?

Explaining Gifted Ed

So again, as a teacher in gifted ed, you must become comfortable with this label. You will to have to first define

55

it for yourself, because you can count on having to explain it to parents, students, other teachers, possibly a coordinator and other administrators as well. You will have to be able to explain to students how they are identified for the program ("How come I'm in this class and Johnny isn't?"); why their needs cannot be met through traditional instruction; and how your class is different than other classes. You'll want to make sure *for yourself* that the school's selection process identifies students for programs that are targeted for these abilities, and that your strengths as a teacher match what you are assigned to teach.

In Chapter Four we'll outline some tactics for discussing the label with small groups of students. They have a definite right to know why they are in the program they're in, yet they need help putting the label in perspective and making neither more (nor less) out of it than is appropriate. The Student Inventory described in Chapter Two is also your first tool in approaching this issue.

But for now, let's try a few of the possible answers to parents' (and other teachers' and kids') "tough questions" on for size:

LIKELY QUESTIONS & POSSIBLE ANSWERS

"What does gifted really mean? How are children selected for this program?

★ Well, according to the Education Consolidation and Improvement Act passed by Congress in 1981, gifted and talented are terms used to describe kids who have high performance capability in intellectual, creative, artistic, leadership, or specific academic fields.

★ To me, gifted means a student learns considerably differently than most children; is capable of learning more, faster within the structured school setting; and can perform at an outstanding level in some area.

★ The Marland Report[3] identified six categories of gifted and talented children: 1) General intellectual ability, 2) Specific academic aptitude, 3) Creative or Productive thinking, 4) Leadership, 5) Visual or performing arts, 6) Psychomotor.

"How are children selected for this program?"

★ At this school, we include children in the gifted program if (choose the appropriate response): They score in the top 3-5 percent on the Stanford-Binet IQ test, (or) who score at the 95th percentile or above on achievement tests, (or) who are recommended because of artistic, creative, or leadership skills. (Or by some combination of the above!)

★ We select students for this program because they possess unusual academic or creative potential and require opportunities not available in the regular classroom. We use a combination of teacher and parent recommendations along with achievement and ability tests.

"How come Joey (Janey's brother) didn't get picked for the program?"

★ I don't know Joey so I can't tell you why he isn't in the program. I do know *Janey,* and she's in the program because . . .

★ Joey may do well on classroom tests, and that's really good. This program, however, was developed for people with high overall learning potential, as measured in intellectual ability tests (such as the Stanford-Binet or the SOI (Structure of the Intellect). The difference between achievement and ability is that achievement tests measure only what you have learned, only what you have been taught. Ability tests measure what you are *capable* of learning (in certain areas). If Joey is working up to his potential and scoring well on classroom tests, he is probably in the right setting.

★ Well, it's probably because Janey scored higher on some tests of general ability, or on tests of creativity or achievement. Although no test is perfect, and we're still learning a lot about how to identify children with special talents, these tests (in combination with other criteria) are the best we have to go on today.

"What's the best way to teach students with high ability? Isn't it better for them to stay in the regular classroom?"

★ Depending on the child, her age, maturity, and type of ability, it may be best to accelerate her in a particular subject, or for an entire grade; or, she may need her curriculum supplemented with enrichment classes. The appropriate option will depend on the type and degree of ability she has and what we as a school have to offer.

★ A "pull-out" or "cluster" class for only gifted kids may be best if a student is ready to go on and work deeper, at higher levels, for longer periods of time. Gifted students who remain in regular classes typically do not get enough of a "workout." They get bored, frustrated, and can suffer emotionally as well as intellectually. Some develop behavior problems. Others fail school, or fail to make connections with meaningful work and friends.

★ Kids at this level of ability simply learn faster and have different learning needs than other students. They need different materials, different kinds of supervision, and different goals set for them. They are also ready to work more on process skills, such as critical thinking and learning skills. Finally, it's important for them to be with other students like themselves—kids who share their interests, who are closer to their mental age than their actual peers. For these reasons, it's best to provide a separate class for them.

"What will my child be learning or doing differently in this gifted program?"

★ Depending on the options chosen for the particular child, he may work in an advanced class or with advanced materials; he may work on projects demanding higher-level thinking skills, or special creative, musical, or problem-solving skills.

★ In addition to more rigorous courses or a broader curriculum (more unusual course selections), students in this program are expected to take more responsibility for their learning. They are expected to help set goals, monitor their own learning, and manage independent time.

★ The work in this class is demanding: we cover more complex concepts in greater depth, and require several kinds of "products" or assignments from students. We encourage them to work in a range of media or presentation modes, such as writing, speaking, music, a staged or filmed documentary, and audiovisuals.

Should I tell my child he or she is gifted?

★ Yes. Depending on the age of the student, explain that he did very well on a particular test, or that he's been recommended for the program because of his work (performance or whatever) in a certain area. Show that you are happy or pleased for him, but limit your expectations to current learning (e.g., "It sounds like a good opportunity for you—I hope you like it.") rather than future burdens (e.g., "You should really be able to make something of yourself now.").

★ Yes. Tell her that the class is designed for kids who learn particularly well in Math (or English, Science, or whatever) and that you're really proud of her for qualifying.

★ Yes. Tell the children how they were selected for the program and that teachers are finding that some kids need extra enrichment classes to think about subjects deeply, or explore projects in a number of different ways. Explain that they may also find more students with similar interests in the class.

"How do I cope with the feelings (i.e., jealousy) of other siblings in our family (or other children in my class) who aren't selected for the gifted program?"

★ Focus on the individual differences and achievements of both (all) children.

★ Show each child that he or she is valued—that many different qualities are extremely desirable and valued (e.g., humor, spirit, honesty, loyalty, industry, caring).

★ Save some of your praise for the gifted child to deliver in private; reinforce all children equally in public.

★ Make sure you give each child as much one-on-one time as possible—don't let the gifted child's talent take up all your time.

"Are YOU gifted?"

★ Yes.

★ No.

★ I don't really know, but I suspect that I may be in some areas.

★ I would probably come out very close to the top in math, but I'm only average in other subjects.

★ I'd like to think I'm a gifted teacher, but they haven't devised a test to measure that yet!

★ Children weren't tested in exactly this way when I was growing up, but yes, somehow I've always known (people have always told me) that I was unusually talented or bright.

★ I've always been a high academic achiever, but my IQ is not in the gifted range, so it's hard to say. I think I'm gifted in some things.

(Other Teachers): "It must be nice having all the smart kids . . .

★ I do really like these kids. They are a real challenge for me, however.

★ (Depending on how the remark is said): Gee, it really makes me mad to hear that. It suggests I don't work as hard as you, when in fact I work very hard. What are you really saying to me?

★ I do have some pretty unusual kids in my class but I'm sure I don't have all the smart ones—there are plenty in other classes too! Besides, all kids have something to offer.

★ It's very different working with the gifted. They can be extremely demanding, and they don't automatically succeed at everything they do.

Teacher: "Mary isn't doing very well in my class this year. Are you sure she belongs in your gifted program?"

★ Have you talked to Mary about her performance in your class?

★ Well, gifted students aren't usually exceptional in everything they do, and math has never been Mary's strong point.

★ Oh, really? What makes you say that?

★ Would you like to sit down with me and Mary and discuss this?

★ Are you sure Mary needs to do the work you're assigning her? Is it something she could test out of, or do an independent study on?

It may be important for you to think some of these issues out by writing down the most frequent questions you get, and experimenting with different answers. Imagine all the parents who've ever confronted you: What were they asking you? What were they worried about? What did they really want to know or be told? Think through additional questions from teachers and administrators: What are the tough questions or comments you get from colleagues? What do students ask you in the hall about the program?

A Teacher Inventory

You may already know which aspects of the gifted ed movement—the program or your role—cause you personal confusion or conflict. If you're not confused or stressed, you're probably in a minority!

Do you wonder—or worry about—whether you are gifted? Are you fairly confident in your teaching ability? Are you comfortable with your school's selection criteria or process? Are you frustrated by a lack of support for the program from the administration and teachers? Are there not enough hours in the days to accomplish all the tasks of your job?

In the Appendix you'll find a Teacher Inventory we developed as a think piece: a way for you to focus on attitudes you have about giftedness and concerns about working with gifted students. Try filling it out like a diary or journal you'd want to read in another five years. And write honestly what's on your mind—what do you know or believe to be true from experience? What do you know or believe on a gut level? What personally makes sense? Even if you're feeling fairly comfortable with your role, don't skip this inventory! Your responses will help prepare you for the activities in Chapter Four.

"Good" Gifted Ed Teachers

Contrary to what you might expect, veteran teachers of the gifted tell us that what is needed most of all to survive in gifted ed is a sense of humor. Humor, plus a strong self-concept, a high energy level, and a sincere liking for gifted students. Rather than in-depth content knowledge or terrific analytical powers, an underlying commitment to students and an attitude about learning seems to be most essential:

I'm not an expert in anything. What I have to offer is an attitude of lifelong learning. I like to learn anything.

–Elementary Gifted Ed Teacher

Similarly, for the elementary homeroom or enrichment teacher, the ability to "learn along with the students" is probably more important than standing up in front of the class, "disseminating knowledge." "In gifted ed you have 2nd, 3rd, and 4th graders who are content area specialists. They already know more facts than you." What they don't know, necessarily, is how to put things in perspective, how to organize their learning, how to chart where they want to go.

Requirements for successful teaching change somewhat when the classes are subject specific and designed for accelerated students. A high school course in Chinese must be taught by someone competent in that language, and advanced calculus needs a well-versed mathematician. But even here, teachers can expect to be challenged by students. A sense of humor, strong self-concept, and a positive attitude about their own continued learning are the qualities which enable teachers to handle challenges gracefully. Teachers should have a solid mastery over their material, but also know their limitations, and be willing (we would hope eager!) to continuously expand their knowledge.

Aside from the personal qualities mentioned above, several didactic talents may be particularly useful to gifted ed teachers. Primary among these is versatility with a range of teaching strategies. If you heavily favor one mode of teaching, such as lecture-discussion, you may find yourself in trouble! To work with gifted students you need to be very flexible, capable of individualizing instruction and managing small and large group activities as well. Gifted students particularly thrive on student-centered instruction, yet they need variety in their daily instructional diet. You can't assign them to independent study all year long. You'll therefore need to be capable of designing small group discussions, large group projects, tutorials, and other learning activities to foster either content knowledge or process skills.

Good gifted ed teachers also probably have considerable communication skills. By this we mean a whole cluster of "people" skills, including:

★ Observation skills: listening, watching, picking up verbal and nonverbal cues

★ Intuition: sensing needs or issues

★ Empathy: communicating concern and interest

★ Role modeling: demonstrating positive attitudes, appropriate behaviors

★ Verbal presentation skills

★ Writing skills

★ Group leadership and counseling skills

In 1982 Kathnelson and Colley[4] asked students in a special project for gifted and highly able learners (ages six to sixteen) to describe their concept of an ideal teacher. Over 50 percent of the responses listed someone who:

★ Understands them

★ Has a sense of humor

★ Can make learning fun

★ Is cheerful

Mentioned 30 percent of the time is the teacher who:

- ★ Supports and respects them

- ★ Is intelligent

- ★ Is patient

- ★ Is firm with them

- ★ Is flexible

Mentioned only 5 percent to 10 percent of the time is the teacher who:

- ★ Knows the subject

- ★ Explains things carefully

- ★ Is skilled in group processes

It may be that the most relaxed, cheerful, and confident teacher is also most knowledgeable (and can therefore afford to be relaxed and cheerful!), but it's interesting that students pick up on these affective qualities faster than expertise.

Recommendations

The focus of this chapter has been on you, the gifted ed teacher, because your attitudes about yourself, about giftedness (the concept and label), and about your gifted students are fundamental to the strategies we propose. If you are uncomfortable with gifted students, or unsure of what the label does and doesn't mean, then your students will pick up on that discomfort.

We'd like to close this chapter with a few recommendations—these suggestions may be most relevant for the teacher new to gifted ed, although the veteran may find some of them worth hearing again.

Seven Tips
For Gifted Ed Teachers

1. If you don't have specific training in gifted ed, get it—any way you can. If you can take the time and can afford a masters program, do it. If not, try to get whatever in-service training is available. Meanwhile, read as much as you can, observe other classrooms or programs, and research your own students.

2. Advocate that *all* staff at your school take at least basic in-service training on the gifted. Everyone should understand more about these students, even if they're working with them for only a few hours a week. (Gifted kids are, after all, gifted 24 hours a day.) You set yourself up for a lot of problems if you allow yourself to become the only "expert" in the house. You'll find that other teachers become more cooperative once they learn more about gifted students and what you're doing with them.

3. Get a support group going for yourself. Don't expect "regular" classroom teachers to provide the support you need — your problems and issues are different. You may actually have more in common with teachers in special services. But isolation is not good: join a network at the district or state level. Form your own informal club, or find a few other gifted ed teachers to talk with routinely.

4. Keep parents informed of your program's goals. Particularly if the program is new, parents will need a certain amount of education. Try to build a strong parent group in the first years, but don't "take over." Let them become responsible for the ongoing management of the group.

You may find parents can be effective advocates and important sources of support if budget cuts or other political issues threaten your program.

5. Give yourself time to grow into your job. Gifted ed teachers have been known to burn out quickly. Many of us suffer from the same need for perfection as our students do, and set unrealistic goals and unreasonable deadlines. Take care of yourself by limiting the number of hours you work overtime. Realize you won't turn underachieving kids around in a year, you can't guarantee each kid will reach her or his potential, and you'll make many of the same "mistakes" other teachers make. (But remember, as one gifted child wrote us, "There's no such thing as a mistake; the only mistake is one not made.") Don't expect miracles from your students; don't expect them from yourself.

6. Give yourself permission to assert yourself and defend your students' rights. Becoming an advocate is not easy. You may feel at odds with a lot of people. Use your support group and parents to help you keep your balance.

7. Enjoy your students; enjoy the subject you're teaching; enjoy your own ability to learn and to grow.

Notes

1. June Cox, Neil Daniel, and Bruce Boston. "Executive Summary," *Educating Able Learners: Programs and Promising Practices* (University of Texas Press, 1985).

2. L. S. Hollingworth, *Children Above 180 IQ* (New York: Arno Press, 1975 [reprint of the 1942 edition]).

3. S. Marland, *Education and the Gifted and Talented* (Washington, D.C.: Commission of Education, 92nd Congress, 2nd Session, USCPO, 1972).

4. A. Kathnelson and L. Colley, "Personal and Professional Characteristics Valued in Teachers of the Gifted" (Unpublished paper presented at California State University, Los Angeles, California, 1982. See Barbara Clark, *Growing Up Gifted,* p. 370.)

4

STRATEGIES: CREATING A SUPPORTIVE ENVIRONMENT

In *Frames of Mind*, Howard Gardner writes of the intrapersonal and the interpersonal intelligences. Intrapersonal intelligence concerns self-knowledge and the ability to discriminate among a range of emotions and needs, and to draw upon this knowledge to guide one's actions. Interpersonal intelligence, in contrast, concerns knowledge of others, and the understanding of how other people's behavior reflects their feelings, attitudes, perceptions, and needs. Both forms of intelligence are necessary for individuals to understand how their personalities and actions affect the group, how the group affects them, and how others perceive them. Without these forms of knowledge, individuals have difficulty mastering their social roles and maturing emotionally.

Gardner points out that societies differ in their approach to and emphasis on personal intelligences. For instance some societies value collective consciousness more than individual focuses, or vice versa. Some cultures explicitly instruct members in self-knowledge or social customs, while others allow individuals to develop personal knowledge and skills on their own through family membership and life experiences. It seems to us that American education, in emphasizing the cognitive over the affective domain, does little to consciously build students' skills in the personal realms, although (as

Gardner says) "emotions and such discriminations clearly involve a cognitive process."[1]

> To feel a certain way—paranoid, envious, jubilant—is to construe a situation in a certain way, to see something as having a possible effect upon oneself or upon other individuals. One may develop appropriate appraisals, finely honed discriminations, accurate categorizations and classifications of situations; or, less happily, one can make excessively gross discriminations, inappropriate labelings, incorrect inferences, and thus fundamentally misinterpret situations. *The less a person understands his own feelings, the more he will fall prey to them.* The less a person understands the feelings, the responses, and the behavior of others, the more likely he will interact inappropriately with them and therefore fail to secure his proper place within the larger community (p. 254).

Gardner is correct; intra- and interpersonal knowledge can emerge naturally through "upbringing," life events, friendships, and the shaping effects of logical consequences (i.e., the consequences of insufficient understanding of self or others). These forms of knowledge can also be obtained through more explicit means such as pyschotherapy, spiritual counseling, self-help books, Dale Carnegie courses and the like, training in psychology, values clarification activities, support groups, or through "literature, rituals, and other symbolic forms." Intra- and interpersonal knowledge can also be elicited by gifted ed (and other) teachers, working directly with personal skills and themes as content, or indirectly, by choosing particular teaching techniques. For example, the Student Inventory presented in Chapter Two is an overt strategy for enhancing students' personal knowledge. Setting up discussion guidelines that promote supportive exchanges and highlight valid differences in opinion (regardless of the topic), is an indirect method of enhancing social knowledge and skill.

Personal intelligence is extremely critical for gifted students because they are already super-sensitive to human dynamics, quick to sense the incongruity of adult behavior, the hidden agendas, the contradictory meanings, the need for personal control or power. Yet they may not know how to interpret these dynamics, much less respond to them. They don't know how to see themselves as peers and family see them; they may feel a mystery unto themselves. Knowledge of self (the conflicts from within) and of others (the conflicts from without) are the important keys to growing emotionally and socially.

Creating a Supportive Environment

You may feel like there's not enough time in the day to add an entirely new component (i.e., personal intelligence or affective education) into the curriculum, but it's already there anyway. You may not be addressing emotional issues directly, but indirectly you're already sending messages that guide or impede students' search for self-knowledge — messages that broaden students' understanding of others or not.

One reason we've provided you with a lot of background on the gifted and asked you to inventory your own needs and feelings as teachers is because this knowledge of yourself and your students is vital in determining how you behave every day in the classroom. A supportive attitude is built into (or not) small things you do every day—gestures, remarks you make "on the fly," physical contact, eye contact, comments written on paper, instructions. To communicate expectations clearly, to give honest and supportive feedback, to reward learning processes as well as products, to involve students in decisions, to take time to listen, to see yourself as facilitator and not just "knowledge disseminator"—all these attitudes and techniques affect student's emotional well-being as much as (or more than) any single group discussion of feelings. Certainly, they go together.

Creating a supportive environment begins the first moment of the first day when students walk into the classroom, and runs concurrently with every instructional task you undertake. Support stems from truly liking the gifted student and enjoying his or her learning style and appetite. But support involves more than smiling, showing enthusiasm, and offering words of encouragement — although these are requisite ingredients. Support is also conveyed by setting clear expectations, giving constructive criticism, being honest, flexible, and providing structure, tangible rewards, comfortable classrooms, accommodating schedules, and routine times for sharing or relaxing.

Listed below, then, are some primary elements to consider when creating a supportive environment for gifted students. If some of them appear obvious, consider how often you put them into practice. Do you periodically check out how well you're coming across in these areas? Some of the most simple strategies are also the best, if we could truly work them into our daily routine.

★ **Your role as teacher:** Basic teaching style, power issues, student autonomy, responsibility for learning

★ **Expectations:** Yours, theirs; ground rules

★ **Rewards:** Behavior you reinforce and how; types of feedback; course credits

Role As Teacher

1. Facilitators and Lecturers

Purpose: To clarify your teaching style and introduce the notion of responsibility for learning.

Strategy: Group discussion.

Procedures: Read students the famous phrase:

> *"Give a man a fish, he eats for a day; teach a man how to fish, he eats for a lifetime."**

Ask students to talk about this in terms of knowledge and learning: Is it more important for teachers to tell students the facts, the answers ("knowledge"), or to teach them how to learn facts and answers for themselves? Generally, we know that knowledge is "exploding" so fast the information we learn today will be out-of-date before long. Many specific jobs and careers will require different sets of knowledge and even different skills by the time students are ready to enter the work force. We also know that people's memories are limited, and learning itself can be a pleasurable process. These are arguments for "learning how to learn." Ask students if they can think of other arguments—both pro and con. Ask them if they have already experienced learning something only to find it out-of-date. Perhaps their parents have changed jobs, gone back to school, or been retrained by their company.

Discussion:

A human being needs both a fish to satisfy his or her immediate hunger, and needs to learn how to fish to survive beyond the day. Similarly, students need to know

*(Although the original author refers to "man," we interpret his meaning to include all human beings.)

certain facts, concepts, and procedures, but they need to learn how to learn and think on their own.

Ask students what they think your job as teacher entails, and what their job as learners is. Are you to give students the information they need in order to progress, but also to teach (or encourage) them to learn on their own? Should students learn how to ask questions, analyze problems, research topics, evaluate their own work and the thinking of others? Should students try to just memorize what the teacher says is important? Talk about how teachers can communicate information and function as a resource and coach at the same time.

Note: Again, try to articulate whatever role you define for yourself. You may wish to let them know your limits, e.g., "I make mistakes too; I have strengths in these particular areas but I don't know everything." This discussion can also serve as a nice introduction to the issue of expectations and students' responsibility for learning.

Expectations (Yours, Theirs)

2. Tangible and Intangible Outcomes

Purpose: To state as clearly as possible what you expect students to do in your class.

Procedures: At the beginning of the year (semester, or even week) prepare a handout for students explaining what you expect them to do, and what you hope to accomplish. Make sure you state your expectations in terms of:

A. Learning Objectives (see samples below)

☆ Understand the components of a research paper

☆ Master the procedures for dissecting vertibrates and invertibrates

☆ Communicate ideas and feeling about one's own ethnic culture in a creative project

☆ Compare autocratic and democratic decision-making

B. Content

☆ Reading assignments (titles, page numbers)
☆ Films or tapes to review

C. Products

☆ What's due, when

D. Methods

☆ How students are supposed to proceed
☆ Overall schedule with list of activities

E. Evaluations

☆ Type (self-evaluation, teacher comments, tests)
☆ Purpose of measures
☆ Policies such as those regarding retests

F. Intangible Outcomes

☆ To start from wherever you are and make progress
☆ To make work personally meaningful
☆ To feel pride in self and in group
☆ To compete in state spelling competition.

Discussion:

Go over the handout and allow students time to ask questions. If possible, indicate options they may have under content, products, and evaluations. For instance, they may choose to work with different content or materials, or pick from three suggested final projects: prepare a photo essay or stage a debate, write a paper, or some other project. Indicate how you want students to negotiate with you for different options, and at what time.

When addressing intangible outcomes, try to express what signs of learning are really most meaningful to you— what you would be most pleased to see in students and what you can realistically expect. This is where understanding your own expectations of gifted students comes into play; be as fair and honest in your expectations as you can.

Also check out expectations students may have of you or the class. See if there are other topics they'd like to cover, other methods or materials they'd prefer to use.

Note: Stating objectives and expectations explicitly for students has known impact on their learning. Given this overview of where they're going and what they're responsible for, they can focus their learning energy better and evaluate their own progress.

Even when assignments are "open" and evaluation consists of measures other than grades or tests, teachers (and other adults) still have expectations—we just take them for granted or assume kids understand them. Making your expectations known causes a stir at first, but public goals cause less anxiety in the long run than hidden or ambiguous goals.

Alleviating the concerns students have about assignments, grades, grading criteria, team assignments, books, and other materials helps build a supportive atmosphere. Checking for these concerns should be done periodically if not almost every session.

3. Ground Rules

Purpose: To make students more aware of how to behave in a group; to improve social skills; to develop a trusting atmosphere.

Procedure: The following ground rules can be prepared ahead of time on a chart and posted, listed on a handout, or elicited (along with student suggestions) in a group discussion. More important than how the rules are first generated and publicized is how they are reinforced. You'll have to look for opportunities to demonstrate, as a role model, ways to respond to criticism, ways to give criticism, and ways to respect someone's privacy. What follows are some sample items that may go on your list; they illustrate the kinds of ground rules we have in mind.

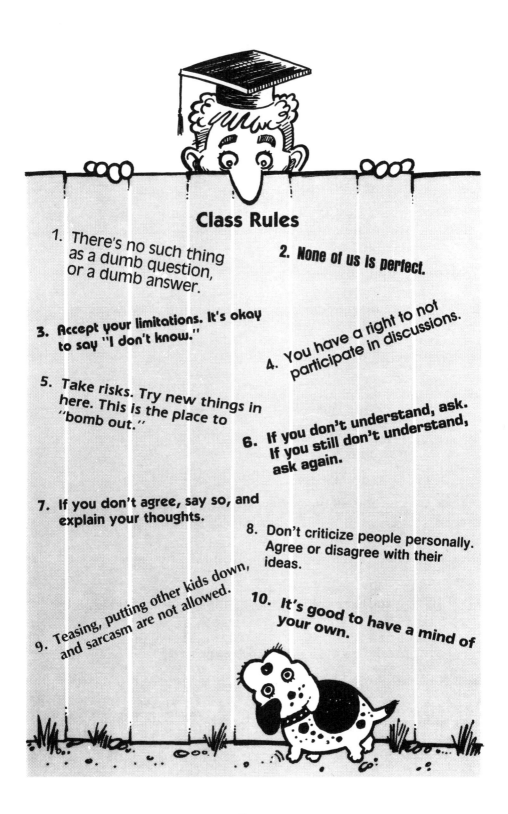

Class Rules

1. There's no such thing as a dumb question, or a dumb answer.

2. None of us is perfect.

3. Accept your limitations. It's okay to say "I don't know."

4. You have a right to not participate in discussions.

5. Take risks. Try new things in here. This is the place to "bomb out."

6. If you don't understand, ask. If you still don't understand, ask again.

7. If you don't agree, say so, and explain your thoughts.

8. Don't criticize people personally. Agree or disagree with their ideas.

9. Teasing, putting other kids down, and sarcasm are not allowed.

10. It's good to have a mind of your own.

Rewards

4. What to Reward and How

Purpose: To determine the kinds of student behavior (other than compliance, perfect test scores, or homework), you want to reinforce, and statements which reinforce them.

Strategy: Observation and planning.

Procedure: Observe your students for several days, noting the behaviors you'd like to reward and those you'd like to discourage. Write these out in a list, then include any other behaviors you can think of which may not have surfaced during your observations. Think about this collection of behaviors; if you wish, share it with another teacher in your gifted network. Here are examples of what we mean:

☆ **Following through on tasks**

☆ **Sharing something personally meaningful**

☆ **Supporting a friend**

☆ **Time on task**

☆ **Asking good questions**

☆ **Taking initiative**

☆ **Demonstrating patience, or self-control**

☆ **Exploring something new**

☆ **Appropriate use of humor**

Your list could well go on and on! Now list ways you can reward students who demonstrate this kind of behavior. Keep in mind several mechanisms for reward, such as:

Positive Reinforcements

☆ Praise   ☆ A hug, or touch on shoulder

☆ Public recognition   ☆ Formal awards

- ☆ Permission to do other things
- ☆ Invitation to present work at parent night or variety show
- ☆ Special class events (speakers, films, field trips)
- ☆ Invitation to "collaborate" with you or another mentor
- ☆ Thank-you notes (public or private)
- ☆ Class celebrations
- ☆ Free time
- ☆ Individual attention
- ☆ Red-letter day
- ☆ Roster of "stars"
- ☆ Progress charts

After you have observed and listed behaviors to reinforce, write out (and then try out!) some corresponding verbal statements.

Verbal Messages That Reinforce

1. (When presented with a report card showing all A's):
   "This looks like you've learned a lot. How do you feel about these marks?"
2. "I'm glad you're helping your buddy out."
3. "You tried something new today—that took courage."
4. "Congratulations on finishing this."
5. "I think this group is ready for the state spelling championships."
6. "You did a good job of standing up for yourself in that discussion."
7. "I'm glad you asked that question because I bet there are ten other people who want to know the same thing."
8. "I believe you can do it."
9. "I think it's great how you took the initiative to . . ."
10. "You showed a lot of patience (or compassion, or self-control) today."

Discussion:

Gifted students need lots of reinforcement for simply being, for relating to one another in mature ways, for relaxing, showing compassion, following through, or taking criticism well. They need straightforward feedback on their accomplishments as well, but they need to get positive feedback on demonstrations of positive social behaviors and other attitudes, too.

One additional point you may want to check on immediately: Some gifted classes don't "count" in terms of credit. Depending on the type of class you have, the number of hours and types of work accomplished, this may be very inappropriate and discriminatory. Gifted students should not have to complete all required coursework and activities on top of their gifted classes for no additional credit. Participation in advanced or enriched classes should be rewarded; otherwise, some kids regard gifted ed opportunities as a punishment for being bright.

Notes

1. Howard Gardner, *Frames of Mind,* (New York: Basic Books, Inc., 1983), p. 254.

5

STRATEGIES: INDIVIDUAL COUNSELING AND ACTIVITIES

For the classroom teacher who needs or chooses to work with students individually on social or emotional issues, several alternative strategies can be developed. These strategies can be used in combination with focus group discussions as well as ongoing support exercises. Or, they can be targeted for students with particularly difficult or unique needs; for those who don't respond well in groups; or for students working in one-on-one situations. The strategies are:

★ **Surveys**

★ **Journals**

★ **Weekly conferences**

★ **Growth contracts**

★ **Peer alliances**

★ **Referral to counseling**

Surveys

Asking students to complete the Student Inventory (see Appendix) is one way to establish the terrain of inter- and intrapersonal knowledge as a legitimate area to investigate and discuss. In fact, the legitimizing function of the Inventory may be its most important outcome. The answers you get may not seem terrifically revealing, particularly the first time around, but that doesn't mean the questions aren't making an impact. Students aren't generally encouraged to clarify their feelings—they're probably not used to identifying conflicts, sources of stress or support. Further, kids who feel uncomfortable with this process may ridicule the task as "unnecessary" or "silly." Yet for students to mature emotionally they need to examine their perceptions, even when it is painful. Posing the questions via the Inventory is a good first step; it stimulates thinking in a relatively safe way and requires no public response.

Surveying students is, in general, a good strategy for getting individuals to address sensitive questions. Unlike open class voting (which is a useful group strategy), questionnaires demand anonymous yet personal answers, and they can be much more explicit. You may wish to instigate very brief weekly surveys on questions concerning academic pressures, careers, or social pressures, and post the results. For example: "In answer to last week's survey on choosing a career, 78 percent of the girls anticipate having a full-time job outside the home as adults, compared to 99 percent of the boys." Again, surveys can engage students individually to reflect on personal traits, values, and attitudes.

A variation on the idea of surveys is illustrated in *100 Ways to Enhance Self-Concept in the Classroom* by Jack Canfield and Harold Wells.[1] Strategy #62, "Weekly Reaction Sheets," consists of quick, ten-item inventories that help students examine how they are using their time. Some sample questions: "What was the high point of the week?" "What did you procrastinate about?" "What unfinished personal business do you have left?" After six weeks of recording their weekly reactions, students are ready for a discussion on what they've learned. By changing the focus of the content, you can use weekly reaction sheets to address a broad range of growth issues.

Journals

The possibilities for personal growth are almost unlimited when journal writing is approached as creative self-examination. Frequent, private writing has both therapeutic and technical value (in terms of language skills development—although journals shouldn't be assigned for this reason). Journals have become quite commonplace in classrooms but their real benefits aren't always tapped. Oftentimes, inadequate direction is given to students (e.g., "Write something down every day"; "Write about anything, just make it at least three lines long"). Lacking the drama of Anne Frank's story, students quickly become bored with the tedium of their lives and of their writing!

Fortunately, there are several concrete journal techniques which give enough form and direction to the process to make the writing revelatory—even without the drama. (More about this in a minute.)

Unlike surveys, journals require individual readings from teachers and some sort of personal response, preferably in writing. Teachers reading student diaries should respond to each entry with a simple statement which acknowledges the student's feeling without judging it. The equivalent, in spoken counseling, is "Yeah, I hear you: it sounds like . . . " Or, you may wish to provide other comments, suggestions, words of encouragement, or drawings.

Because responding individually to student journals takes time, you may need to limit the number of times you assign journals, or to assign them only to students who seem to enjoy them the most. Journals may work best for students who already enjoy writing, or who seem inclined to introspection. A shy student who tends to observe rather than participate may flower with this type of individual assignment. We do not believe journals should be graded. Neither should they be required if, after a mandatory trial period, they seem unnecessary, duplicative, or nonproductive for the writer.

An excellent source for journal techniques is *The New Diary* written by Tristine Rainer.[2] Rainer lists four basic diary devices; these are "natural modes of expression" which serve different purposes of writing for oneself. They are:

1. **Catharsis.** This consists of emotional out-pouring, a let-loose, tell-it-like-it-is outburst of intense feelings. The focus is not on objective reporting or analysis of joy, anger, jealousy, or melancholy (that comes later), but simply on expressing the feeling.

2. **Description.** In contrast to catharsis, this device calls for a reality-based rendition of events and scenes as perceived by the writer. Here, events, places, and people that are important to the writer can be selected out and highlighted with personal comments.

3. **Free-intuitive.** This third device springs from deeper consciousness. Language from this mode is comprised of abstract, unedited, "free associations of the mind." This form of writing expresses the immediate present— what is current on the writer's mind—and can be helpful for overcoming writer's blocks. People who are interested in language, psychology, and the unconscious often find stream-of-consciousness writing most intriguing.

4. **Reflection.** With this final device the writer engages in retrospection. After taking a semi-detached perspective, the author recalls the past in order to analyze and synthesize events.

These four modes of expression can be translated into guided assignments for the diarist (if guidance is needed) or simply presented so students can expand upon already established styles. For hesitant students, Rainer also describes seven specific techniques for triggering writing, from "list-making" to "portraiture," from "altered points of view" to "secret buddies" and "unsent letters."

Although many of these devices would be useful to any student, some may be particularly provocative for gifted students trying to come to terms with their differences. For instance, ask a gifted student to:

Journal Entry Ideas

☆ Write an entry from the point of view of someone not in the gifted program

☆ List your favorites: e.g., books, songs, food, clothes

☆ Describe traits of an imaginary friend

☆ Compose a portrait of yourself as you are now and as you expect to be in ten years

☆ Describe a tranquil, beautiful, or particularly stimulating place to be; invent an episode which could take place there

☆ Reconstruct an angry dialog you had with a friend or relative

☆ Write an imaginary conversation with a favorite (talking) pet

---

Journal assignments can be supplemented by readings from other famous diarists such as Franz Kafka, Anais Nin, and Anne Frank. Some autobiographies also provide excellent models of journal-style approaches, for instance *The Autobiography of Malcolm X*, journalist Eric Sevaried's autobiography, *Not So Wild a Dream*, or the famous novels by Joy Adamson about Elsa, the lion. Gerrald Durrell's autobiography *My Family and Other Animals* is a delightful account of growing up (a naturalist and precocious zoologist) with a wildly talented and humorous family on the island of Corfu. Students benefit not only from the content of these authors' lives, they again gain permission to travel "inside their heads" in pursuit of self-knowledge. Such authors can also function as positive role models or mentors for students.

Your librarian can help identify other diaries and autobiographies which gifted students may particularly enjoy. Also, the *Gifted Children Newsletter* (December, 1982) suggests two additional sources of "therapeutic" literature: *The Bookfinder: A Guide to Children's Literature About the Needs and Problems of Youth* (ages 2–15) by Sharon S. Dryer (American Guidance Service, Circle Pines, Minnesota, 1981); and *Books for the Gifted Child* by Barbara Baskin and Karen Harris (Bowker, New York, 1980).

Weekly Conferences

Weekly conferences may provide just the right amount of attention, in just the right format, for certain students in need of temporary or periodic counseling. Naturally, if the student has serious emotional or psychological problems, he needs to see a professional counselor in addition to talking with you. But as a classroom or special services teacher you should be rightfully concerned if a student is having trouble in your class. And before you refer a student to someone else, the weekly conference is a good first recourse. Regular office hours can be set up after school for any student to visit you on an as-needed, first-come, first-served basis. Or, you can ask particular students to come in for scheduled appointments.

The purpose of student conferences changes, of course, with the student. For some kids, the issue may be breaking away emotionally from parents who don't understand their need to be independent. (Independence, for them, may be symbolized by being different, or by being totally average! A kid who's been pushed too hard for too long will assert his independence by being "ordinary.") For others it may be trying to rekindle interest in school, or slowing down and focusing on only a few tasks at once. For others, it may be the pressure of grades, lack of friends, or lack of role models. They may be weighted down by heavy-duty expectations, or multiple college or career options. The outcomes of your conference will vary from improving their academic performance, to tempering their productivity; from changing (or individualizing) assignments, to recommending extra-curricular activities or psychological testing. Although the specific goal will change from student to student, individual conferences can accomplish several things.

1. Give kids a chance to ventilate beyond group discussions (which they may not be participating in fully anyway) whatever personal problems are interfering with their work or life.

2. Give you a chance to confront a student whose grades or level of participation is slipping; the student who is becoming increasingly negative; the student who seems anxious and depressed. Confrontation in this sense means getting out the message: "I see that something is going on with you. Will you tell me about it? We're going to have to work something out here . . . . " The act of intervention alone tells the depressed kid his feelings have been noticed; the irresponsible kid his "act" isn't fooling anyone. It tells the passive kid his lack of participation is cause for concern.

3. Indicate that you care about the student as a person by listening and taking his feelings seriously.

4. Problem-solve different solutions.

5. Provide direction and support as students go about implementing solutions.

Condensed guidelines for weekly conferences are difficult to give when the issues at stake, and the age and type of learner are so variable. But perhaps the simple approach described here will lend direction to your already evolving practices. Keep in mind the common problems of gifted students. Keep in mind their particular need for self-knowledge, need for acceptance and understanding of others. Your observations, questions, feedback, and your affirmation of them as people will help them gain these forms of knowledge. Specifically, you may wish to:

1. Use the first session (or two or three) as a time to "get the full story"— to listen to and understand the student's perception of herself, her conflicts and all that is related.

2. Clarify what you (the teacher) feel may be misperceptions on the student's part. As the excerpt from Gardner stated (see Chapter Four), feelings are partially dependent upon cognitive reasoning. They are based on perceptions and assumptions which may or may not be correct. Ask the student to clarify fuzzy statements by rephrasing them, and asking for examples and verification.

3. Suggest ways a student might test her perceptions out. For instance: "Have you asked your mother directly whether she cares about you attending an Eastern college?" "If you're convinced the English teacher thinks you can't write, perhaps you ought to ask for a conference and get a fuller evaluation." "You say other kids don't like you. Is there any way you could test that conclusion out?"

4. Ask the student what he wants to do about the problem, what he would like to see happen.

5. Get a sense of when the student is ready to think about solutions. Even after gathering new information and new insights into a problem, the student may not be ready to let go of it. Chronic problems can, in particular, give people a sense of identity, and changing them (or changing one's response to them) can

cause anxiety. But when students seem ready to admit there just might be a solution to their problem, brainstorm like crazy. Back up the ideas with measurable goals, concrete plans, and dates for keeping in touch. During the follow-up conferences, find out what happened: Did the solution work? Why or why not? Does the strategy need readjustment? Or does the problem need to be reanalyzed and redefined?

6. Set behavioral guidelines for some students while they work on problems that can't change overnight. Students may not be ready to work on solutions for some time, but they still need to conform to certain expectations in the meantime. For example, it may take years to turn a really discouraged kid around. Perhaps the underlying problem is perfectionism, transfigured into fear of failure. You meet with him regularly to reinforce his efforts, and to reinforce your minimum expectations (staying in school, not missing class, maintaining a C average, doing required work, whatever).

7. Ask the student what she is learning about herself by having this conflict, by experiencing the emotions it causes, by examining the perceptions she forms, and testing the solutions she generates. Conflict in life is not always avoidable. What matters is how she deals with it and uses it to grow internally. Some of our greatest opportunities for growth come from conflict, if we only have the courage to meet it with both eyes open.

If deeply-rooted issues such as chemical dependency, family conflict, child abuse, or suicidal feelings emerge, refer the student to more formal evaluation and make sure it happens. Continue to be a listener and an advocate, but demand honesty. You may not be the person to work with her on a deeper emotional level, but you can at least confront her on behavior in your class, and her delusions—"I may not know the answer to your problem, Sharon, but you and I both know that's not true." You can also reinforce her for the positive steps she takes. Stay committed to your course of action, which is to observe, set limits, provide encouragement, respond to needs when possible, and tell the truth.

Growth Contracts

Growth contracts are written agreements between individual students and teachers, specifying a plan for personal change or growth within a set period of time. Goals generally focus on affective issues of concern to the student. In this respect they differ from learning contracts which are essentially academic. (Changing one's *attitude* about school, or improving performance in a particular area would be an appropriate growth contract goal, however.) Both the high achiever, wishing to meet new friends, and the underachiever, wanting to find something that holds his or her interest (a goal which inevitably involves risk-taking), can benefit from the process of setting intentions and strategies down on paper.

Growth contract time lines may be as short as one week or as long as a year. Contracts can be initiated by either the student or the teacher. Whether you'll require them of all students, use them only with kids meeting with you for weekly conferences, or for a single student in a special situation will depend upon your own set of circumstances.

One key to making growth contracts successful is helping the student to articulate something that is really important to him or her. The goal of the contract should reflect a felt need. A second key consists of finding strategies that are reasonably small and concrete, and easy to monitor and evaluate. The third key is time commitment from you: the teacher must stay involved. Even the most motivated student needs the reinforcement of having someone to talk to about his or her progress and problems.

Growth Contract

1. *Target area for growth: "Something I want to change about myself or my life. "I'd like to be . . ."*

2. *Steps I'll take to reach my goal . . .*
   a.
   b.
   c.

3. *Resources that will help me along the way (including people for support) . . .*
   a.
   b.
   c.

4. *Roadblocks to get around . . .*
   a.
   b.
   c.

5. *Evaluation: How will I know when things are better? "I'll know when . . ." How close to this goal did I come? Did I achieve as much as I'd expected? Did I achieve less than I'd hoped?*

Some suggested questions to use in discussing progress on the contract are:

1. How easy or how difficult for you is (was) it to work on this contract?

2. Is the goal still worthwhile to you? Have other goals replaced it?

3. If you had to do this over, would you take different steps? Why or why not?

4. Do you need to think of other ways to overcome these obstacles? What can you do? Who can help you?

5. What has come as the biggest surprise to you, working on this contract?

6. How do you feel about the reactions you've been getting from other people, now that you are making these changes?

7. How are you feeling about yourself these days?

8. Do you remember how you felt in the beginning? Have there been any changes?

In summary, keep in mind that whether students fulfill their contracts down to the letter is less important than the information and skills they gain in the process. Achieving complete success is wonderful—but any measure of progress is worth celebrating. Meanwhile, setting goals, designing strategies to meet those goals, working on those strategies, improvising, and seeing what works are skills students will use throughout their lives in an infinite number of settings.

Peer Alliances

For the gifted student who is emotionally troubled, socially "ungifted" or withdrawn, large groups may seem safe because they're large. Small groups seem threatening when sharing and participation are required, and one-to-one partnerships the most threatening of all. But small groups and peer teaching (or "alliances") may also give the loner the individual attention he needs. They may offer the best, most private arena for him to try out his newly acquired social skills and to learn about other people.

Partnerships can be short-term (limited to the length of one learning project or exercise), or long-term (as with a year-long study partner). They can be formed between students at the same academic or age level, or between students of different ages and abilities. Tutoring younger or less-advanced students is a good variation of one-to-one learning.

Using assigned partners or small teams (of three or four members) can build social awareness and skills either directly or indirectly. If addressing communication skills, values, attitudes, or feelings directly, start partners off with low-risk activities and work toward exercises requiring more intimacy and self-disclosure. Several factors seem to affect the success of the peer alliances:

1. *Compatibility of members.* Age, sex, and personalities are all important. Students of various ages can be grouped together but not indiscriminately.

2. *Awareness of ground rules for working together.* Students can help develop these rules. They usually appreciate having established guidelines.

3. *Length of time allowed for the relationship to develop.* Kids can't become close immediately just because they're gifted.

4. *Expected outcomes of the alliance.* Not all partners will necessarily benefit or get along. Determine in your own mind what minimum outcomes you're looking for.

When given the option, kids usually rush to be with their friends when choosing small groups or partners. As you know, this is not always a good thing! Use your discretion when placing students together; ideally their strengths and limitations should balance each other out. They should have some rapport (or the potential for it) but not be so close as to preclude any challenge or opportunity for new experiences.

Think ahead of time about guidelines your students will need, to work together productively. How long will the students be working together? What is the purpose of the alliance, the task? What terms will they have to work out themselves (such as division of labor, agreement of topics or methods), and what will they need to work out with you? What do they do when they get stuck?

Keep in mind that short-term partnerships are very useful for serving immediate purposes, but they won't make long-term changes in a withdrawn or antisocial student. You may not always be able to find the right person to team up with a particularly lonely, socially inept kid, but when you do, give them enough time to get to work with and know each other. On the other hand, don't be afraid to terminate a partnership that isn't doing either student any good.

Ask yourself what you expect to happen for the students as a result of the alliance: Better study habits? More confidence? A friendship? Learning to work in a team? Support for each other? What are the signs of success, and the symptoms of dysfunction?

Activities to Strengthen Partnerships

One good exercise for developing feelings of friendship between partners is the "Trust Walk." Many variations of this activity exist, but we favor one by Canfield and Wells.[1] One partner leads the other around the room (or the building) with her eyes closed, then they switch places, and later talk about the experience of having to depend on the other person. You can ask them: Was it easier to lead, or easier to be led? Which role was preferable? Why?

A second activity that focuses on communication skill is described by Diane Brode.[3] Students sit back-to-back and draw imaginary animals without letting their partner see their drawing. Then, they are each to describe this animal to their partner, still sitting so their drawing is hidden. Questions of clarification are allowed, but not hand motions or peeking! On the basis of the verbal description alone, students must try to redraw their partners' animal. When completed the four drawings are compared, and the difficulties of sending exact messages can be discussed as a group. This exercise demonstrates how difficult it can be to send a clear message, and to listen carefully.

Referral to Counseling

Although this option is last in this section, it by no means should be considered the option of last resort. Referring a student for professional therapy does not mean he's beyond other forms of help, or has even exhausted the alternatives. Therapy is more than a form of treatment for the emotionally conflicted; it is potentially a unique form of education in the interpersonal and intrapersonal realms. Any introspectively inclined person can benefit. Professional individual psychotherapy is undoubtedly one of the best ways gifted students can learn more about themselves and their conflicts with the world—whether these conflicts are severe or not.

But individual (or group) psychotherapy is expensive and not always covered by medical insurance. School psychologists may or may not be qualified or available. In large urban public schools they typically have heavy work loads and limited time. For these reasons alone, you probably should explore a number of options for students in addition to psychological counseling. You probably should also keep in mind that for some students, the referral to therapy itself greatly affects their self-concept. They may see it as a punishment or feel there really is something wrong with them ("I must be really weird")— and therefore doubly ashamed and angry. Others will approach it fearfully but also with relief. Your attitude about therapy is really important; if therapy represents failure or disgrace (either yours or the kid's) it will be more difficult for the student to accept it. It helps if a teacher can say, "I was once helped greatly by a counselor," or "I'm really happy that you're going to be getting some help with this. Good for you for having the courage to work on it."

If your school does not already provide counseling for the gifted, strongly encourage them to do so. The proper arena for support groups for the gifted is really in the counselor's office. Psychologists or counselors are better equipped to sort out the variety of problems in students' lives, whether they're related to the home, career options, finances, drugs, peer group or identity, sex, or school and intellectual concerns. These problems are inevitably intertwined, particularly when one or more is chronic.

As was mentioned in the previous section on weekly conferences, your job will be to maintain contact with the counselor while continuing to meet with the student and problem-solve the school problems together. Resist the temptation to feel overly responsible for your kids. It's easy to become too wrapped up in their lives and affected by their struggles. And although teaching is a caring profession, you'll need to define the limits of your involvement and not feel guilty for doing so. Do not hesitate to refer a student to a professional counselor when you feel there is something going on that needs to be looked at, and which requires more time and more specialized training than you've got.

Notes

1. Jack Canfield and Harold C. Wells, *100 Ways to Enhance Self-Concept in the Classroom* (Englewood Cliffs, New Jersey: Prentice-Hall, 1976), p. 139.
2. Tristine Rainer, *The New Diary: How to Use a Journal for Self-Guidance and Expanded Creativity* (Los Angeles: J. P. Tarcher, Inc., 1978), pp. 51-114.
3. Diane S. Brode, "Group Dynamics With Gifted Adolescents," *Gifted, Creative, Talented* (November/December, 1980), p. 62.

6

STRATEGIES: FOCUS GROUP DISCUSSION

In this chapter we'll present discussion guidelines for the "eight great gripes" of gifted students.

The Eight Great Gripes of Gifted Kids

1. No one explains what being gifted is all about—it's kept a big secret.

2. School is too easy and too boring.

3. Parents, teachers, and friends expect us to be perfect all the time.

4. Friends who really understand us are few and far between.

5. Kids often tease us about being smart.

6. We feel overwhelmed by the number of things we can do in life.

7. We feel different, alienated.

8. We worry about world problems and feel helpless to do anything about them.

STRATEGIES

1. No one explains what being gifted is all about—it's kept a big secret.

Purpose: To review definitions of giftedness, and explain how students qualify for these special programs.

Strategy: Group discussion and handout.

Preparation: Complete the Teacher Inventory and have kids complete the Student Inventory (see Appendix). Gather existing definitions of giftedness including those from your program, other sources, and readings. (See Chapter Three, Tough Questions and Possible Answers.)

Procedure: Ask students to arrange their chairs in a circle (or to sit on the floor). Have each person define giftedness, intelligence, or talent. Keep going until no one can think of another definition or characteristic to add. Do this exercise quickly—ask people to name one definition or element after the other, off the tops of their heads.

   Then pass around a handout in which you have written your program's definition, along with the federal guidelines, and other definitions you have collected and think important.

Discussion Questions:

1) What do you think giftedness means?

2) Is this the only definition there is?

3) How are the definitions on this handout different?

4) Why do you suppose there are so many definitions?

5) Why is giftedness so hard to define?

6) Are gifted people "better" people? How are they different from, and how are they the same as other people?

7) Do people here today understand how or why they were chosen for this program?

8) Do you have any questions about this program or what's expected of you?

9) What expectations do you have of me, your teacher?

Discussion Guidelines:

Be prepared to explain any tests involved with your selection process, as well as the Stanford-Binet IQ test, properties of the normal ("bell-shaped") curve, and the meaning of standard deviations. Also be prepared to deal with questions concerning the reliability and validity of these tests. Zaffran and Colengelo[1] provide a useful summary of test caveats (see below).

General Cautions About Tests

1. Don't confuse testing the performance of pupils with inventorying feelings, attitudes, interests, and what are often called personality traits. Although inventories look like tests they are not tests.

2. Don't try to set up some mythical level of ability from a test score and expect a pupil to work up to that level at all times, in all areas of study.

3. Don't compare a pupil's score with a norm unless there is reason to believe that cultural circumstances are similar.

4. Don't expect too much from tests. They do not measure all of the school's objectives (to say nothing of your own, or the students'). And they provide only a small sample of what they do measure.

5. Don't use a test simply because others do. Don't use one unless it serves one of your purposes.

6. Do use carefully selected tests cautiously. They may help to understand the individual pupil and suggest the next steps in his education.

—Excerpt from Zaffran and Colangelo
Counseling With Gifted and Talented Students[1]

The class may not reach, in one discussion, a consensus on the meaning of giftedness—adults certainly haven't, so we can hardly expect students to! But aim to demystify the word, and to clarify why students are in the class or program. Emphasize that we're still learning a lot about exceptional ability and talent. The label gifted isn't meant to typecast people as much as it is to recommend certain kinds of instruction in certain fields.

You'll want to summarize that gifted people are not "better" people but that other people may be angry about the superiority which the label suggests. Gifted students may be superior academically or in specific areas of talent, but there are many other valuable qualities in human beings, and intellectual or creative abilities are only some of them. How any student develops his or her abilities is what's important, and people at all levels of ability make significant contributions to our world. And finally, the "gift" that they have is theirs, to nurture and share as they can. They don't owe society for having been born with a high potential. They don't owe the world anything more than any other citizen does.

2. School is too easy, too boring.

Purpose: To understand what feelings underlie boredom; to clarify what is boring; to help students acknowledge their responsibility for being bored

Strategy: Individual task, followed by group discussion.

Preparation: Locate several large photographs showing close-ups of a human face. Ideally, each student should have his or her own photo to study, and the selection should include men and women from various ethnic cultures. Life magazine, photography books, and magazine advertisements are all good sources. Xeroxing copies of a good black and white photograph for the entire class would be sufficient as long as the resulting image is graphically clear enough to be compelling.

Procedure: This exercise is composed of two parts. First, you introduce the topic of boredom and find out how prevalent it is among your students (refer to their inventories if you wish). Discuss what they think the causes of boredom are, and their feelings associated with it. Then present them with a task. The task takes at least 15 minutes. A summary discussion follows. Depending on your schedule, you may wish to use two days to complete this exercise.

Part One: Have students take their usual seats or find a comfortable spot. Tell them you will be holding a discussion on the subject of boredom.

Discussion Questions:

1. Does anyone in here ever feel bored?

2. What is that feeling like?

3. Are there other feelings that seem to go along with boredom, such as anger or disappointment? What are they? Can you describe them?

4. When do you feel most bored? Can you predict which things (events, subjects, people, obligations, tasks) will bore you most? Has this type of thing always bored you?

5. What can you do about being bored?

Discussion Guidelines:

Try to get students to look at all the feelings that go along with the phrase, "I'm bored." Kids often say they are bored when they really mean something else, such as "I'm afraid to make the effort," or "I'm lonely," or "I, really don't know how to focus or get involved" or "I'm angry they're making me do this again" or "I'm mad about something unrelated." By probing and rephrasing you should be able to elicit some of these feelings. If they're angry about school-work, they're also probably frustrated and depressed that people don't recognize the work is boring, or don't trust them to work on something more meaningful.

Knowing specifically what is boring is useful self-knowledge. Not everyone will be interested in everything. Try to get students to list very specifically what bores them: Chemistry? School dances? Cars? Television? Math? Basketball? Questions about emotions? Politics? Being told what to do? Being 13-years-old? If "the whole system" bores them, this points to a larger problem involving anger and self-esteem.

Write down the various actions students say they take when they're bored, but hold your comments until the task is over.

Part Two: Instruct students to choose a photograph, study it, and write about the face for 15 minutes. The task is to remain engaged, to keep looking for something interesting in the face, to keep finding something to observe and describe. The "essay" doesn't need a beginning, middle, or end; it won't be judged on literary merit. The exercise is about seeing, and realizing there is always something more there, if one looks long enough. For this reason, the time limit needs to be long enough to stretch people's usual period of concentration. Fifteen minutes may or may not be long enough. When students start looking around as though they are bored, press them to keep looking, keep writing, even when they think they've said it all.

Discussion Questions:

1. What kinds of things did you write about?

2. Did you discover anything about the person's face that surprised you—that you didn't see in the beginning?

3. How many people found it hard to keep writing? Did you reach a point when there seemed to be nothing new to say?

4. For those of you who kept writing, how did you keep yourself involved? What did you do to keep going?

Discussion Guidelines:

Find out and discuss what kinds of observations, descriptions, and stories the students wrote. Were the essays imaginative? Factual? Personal in nature? Emphasize how many different approaches students took with the same exercise. If they all say they were bored, try the exercise again, providing them with more clues on how to stay involved. Examples of more clues might be: "Highlight what you see visually." "Fantasize about the person. What is the person thinking or feeling? What kind of life have they had?"

If students were able to push themselves beyond initial observation and discover something new, reward them! Ask them to relate their discovery, and to describe the feeling it gave them.

The wrap-up for this discussion is, of course, that we are all somewhat responsible for our own boredom. Sometimes our boredom is in direct proportion to the amount of effort or energy we invest with a subject. Typically we choose not to invest much of ourselves in a subject that is difficult, threatening, or simply unappealing, thus automatically lessening the return we might get from it. A constantly bored student may be a fantastically brilliant, accelerated-type learner, but be skeptical! He may also be a floater, not able to risk self-disclosure, failure, or personal energy. What's more, kids today are used to being passively entertained, whereas all the best strategies for combating boredom require action.

Stress concrete steps to take when students are bored. Refer to their own solutions; encourage them to find out more about "uninteresting topics," to take risks by trying new approaches to old problems. Generally, solutions boil down to, "change what you can change; avoid what you really need to avoid; and make it interesting when you can." Reinforce the notion that they have more power over their boredom than they think!

3. Parents, teachers, and friends expect us to be perfect all the time.

Purpose: To discuss sources of perfectionism (self, parents, teachers, "society"); feelings associated with it; ways to handle it.

Strategy: Open-ended group discussion.

Procedures: Arrange students in a circle, introduce the topic, and have students help generate the agenda. Begin by listing two or three agenda items yourself, then request others. Once the discussion gets going, you may want to let other students moderate the discussion. (One at a time, of course!) This gives them a chance to practice leadership skills and also helps the group to focus on itself, rather than looking to you for answers.

Possible Agenda Items:

★ Sources of Perfectionism

★ Feelings Associated with Failure

★ What To Do About Expectations—Ours, and Theirs?

Discussion Questions:

1. Who says you have to be perfect? How do they say it? If the message isn't verbal, how does it come out? Why do you suppose they expect or want you to be perfect?

2. Is it possible to be perfect? In everything? All the time?

3. How perfect do you want to be? What are your standards or goals? Are they realistic, or idealistic? Which should they be?

4. What happens when you're less than perfect? How do you feel when you get answers wrong, or receive less than an A?

5. How many people feel anxious about being "good enough"? How many people worry about their grades?

6. Who should set your performance standards?

7. What answers can you give to people who expect too much?

8. How else can you fortify yourself against unrealistically high expectations—your own, and other people's?

Discussion Guidelines:

In the beginning of the discussion, kids will simply need to ventilate about how everyone else expects unreasonable things from them, values them only when they perform well, or "punishes" them in some manner for poor performance. Let students air their views, but also try to get them to articulate how these expectations are conveyed (have them reality-test their perceptions). Some of the messages they hear may be ambiguous, and some may be unmistakeably clear. (And some may be in their heads!) Periodically summarize for them the sources of this perfectionism and how frequently they hear it.

Get students to explore their intrinsic needs for success and perfection. As we stated in Chapter Two, certain conflicts come from within students, and the need to "get it right" according to their vision and level of complexity may be one of those conflicts. Accustom students to the idea that their own expectations may influence how they perceive other people's expectations, and that their internal goals and needs can be more powerful than others (and more fullfilling) in the long run.

Some of the clues to perfectionism lie in the emotions that accompany "failure" (lack of perfection). What are the consequences of poor performance? Loss of identity? ("She must not be as smart as we thought," or "Perhaps he's not gifted after all.") Heavy guilt and anxiety suggest a deep need to satisfy parents and teachers, and concern about being valued as a person, rather than being valued for high performances. Disappointment and anger suggest a need to satisfy one's own internal standards, and perhaps the inability to admit to certain limitations. ("I can't be gifted if I don't get all A's.") Have students try to name the emotions they feel upon "failing," and ask them to analyze the source of that feeling.

One's defense in the face of perfectionism depends on its source—if parents are the task-masters then students need to understand their parents' feelings (Is it need for paternal fulfillment? Love and concern for the student? Self-aggrandizement?) and find appropriate answers to it. If societal or educator views are the source, then appropriate responses to them need to be found. If the source of conflict is partially or predominantly internal, the student needs to learn how to become his or her own "best friend" or supporter, rather than task-master. Encouragement, support, and careful goal-setting can help here.

4. Friends who really understand us are few and far between.

Purpose: To tell stories about friendship; to contrast loneliness with aloneness, and popularity with friendship.

Strategy: Small group and large group discussions.

Procedures: First, divide the group into three teams. Tell them to elect a captain or spokesperson and remind them of small group discussion ground rules. Each team is to spend ten to fifteen minutes relating personal episodes and stories involving friendship. Then, in the large group, discuss the differences between friendship and popularity, and between aloneness and loneliness.

Instruction to the students for small group discussion: "Each person is to think of an episode, real or imaginary, involving a friend. It can be either a positive or negative episode; you can describe the ideal friend or the worst possible friend. The episode can express what you long for in a friendship, what you fear about friendship, what you don't understand, or regret. Each team member is then to relate the episode to the group. Group members are to listen without interrupting until the speaker is finished. When finished, the group may comment or ask questions about the story."

Discussion Questions (for the teacher to ask when circulating around the small groups):

1. Why did you choose to relate that episode?

2. How many other people have had an episode like that, or imagined that kind of incident?

3. Why do you suppose the friend behaved that way (so rottenly, so generously)?

4. How do you (the speaker) now feel, thinking back on that episode?

5. What kind of friend does that make you want to be?

Once in the large group, ask a couple of students if they would share their episodes. Ask them if they have any additional comments; ask them if they learned about some common feelings and experiences. Then, proceed with expanding on these personal stories with the following task.

Large Group Task (to the teacher): Write on the board (or newsprint tablet) four words: Loneliness/ Aloneness, and Popularity/Friendship, as large headings above blank columns. Tell the students you want to discuss the difference between loneliness and aloneness, and between popularity and friendship. List the attributes of each condition on the board underneath its appropriate heading.

Discussion Questions:

1) How do you feel when you're alone? When you're lonely? What's the same? What's different?

2) Does anyone like being alone? or lonely?

3) Is it possible to be alone without being lonely?

4) How can you tell when other people are lonely?

5) Name some examples of famous people (in history or fiction, film, or whatever) whom you suspect are (or were) lonely, and explain why you chose them.

6) What personal qualities make a good friend? or for a good friendship?

7) What personal qualities make someone popular? Are the qualities the same as those you look for in a good friend? Which characteristics overlap and which are unique?

8) What are the most important qualities for a friend to have? Let's vote . . .

Discussion Guidelines:

Telling tales of friendships past and friendships future is a nice way to ease into some pretty intense feelings. If students need coaxing to open up, however, be ready with an anecdote on friendship of your own to start the group rolling. Or, bring a few passages from literature (fiction or biographies) to serve as examples. (One of our favorites is the chapter entitled "Loneliness" from *Charlotte's Web*, but you'll have to decide what's appropriate for your group.)

Summarize what the groups discover in terms of common human needs. In friendships and groups we seek such things as acceptance, identity, loyalty, support, companionship, advice, laughter, solace, and power. Relate how their episodes underscore any of these human needs.

Some of the sting can be taken out of aloneness if students realize its benefits. Solitude can be a wonderfully creative state; it provides time and space for reflection and integration. Artists, inventors, musicians, writers, and presidents learn to tolerate solitude, and many crave it. Aloneness should not be feared as an unnatural state, for solitude is not a problem; loneliness is.

Remind students that one doesn't necessarily need a lot of friends—one or two close friends may be all that's necessary. Great popularity usually falls to outgoing people who possess qualities others admire and wish to emulate, yet who remain within the range of "normal" or familiar. Popular leaders represent the more dominant values of the group; popular girls look and dress in ways most conforming to group tastes; popular guys use language adopted by the dominant clique. When popularity depends on conformity to norms, this often excludes the highly gifted student.

But sometimes highly popular people are also lonely; they have the acquaintanceship of many and the friendship of none. Friendship should provide a refuge from having to perform, and it should respect difference as well as similarities.

Close by summarizing ways to handle aloneness and loneliness. Recap students' observations regarding good friends; what are those good friends capable of doing? How do they do it? How can we all make better friends? How can we, as a group, help each other out?

5. Kids often tease us about being smart.

Purpose: To learn how to respond to teasing in a nonthreatened, non-threatening way.

Strategy: Discussion and brainstorming.

Procedure: As a group, discuss what teasing is all about, what forms it comes in, and its effects (on the giver and receiver). Next, brainstorm responses to teasing. Conclude with the positive ways to respond to differences.

Group Discussion Questions:

1) Have any of you been teased? What are you teased about? What words or things are said?

2) When people tease you, how do you feel? Is what they say about you accurate and true? Do you have to listen to it and accept it?

3) Do some kinds of teasing feel okay, and other kinds make you extremely furious or upset? What's the difference? Can you give me some examples?

4) Why do you suppose people tease others? What do you suppose is going on inside them, and with their feelings about themselves?

5) Have you ever teased anyone? Someone who was younger, or different? Do you remember why you teased them? How did it make you feel?

6) When someone teases you, either a little or a lot, what do you usually do? What would you like to do? What would you ultimately like to happen about this teasing? (Discuss which applies):

   ★ I just want the teaser to leave me alone

   ★ I'd actually like to be friends with the teaser

   ★ I want the teaser to shut up and respect me

   ★ I'd like to get even—teach the teaser a lesson

   ★ I don't mind the teasing—it helps ease the tension and it's meant in fun

As a group try brainstorming some possible answers for each "outcome" or solution listed above. For instance, students might choose to ignore certain remarks if they want to be left alone; think of something witty or sensibly cool if they want to earn some respect; and invent something equally humiliating if they need revenge. List possible responses on the board and talk about how they sound, what they might accomplish.

The kids could get carried away here playing around with nasty retorts. A little of this might be appropriate, particularly for some shy kids who need practice standing up for themselves. But keep asking/reminding students that what they probably want is to be included, at least respected, or just left alone; inflammatory remarks don't tend to buy you those outcomes. The best defense usually is to not let the teasing "get to" you, to make light of it, or to respond assertively if it continues.

Some suggested responses to teasing:

★ Big deal. Who cares about that?
★ I don't have a problem with that. Do you?
★ Personally, I'm glad I'm different.
★ Frankly, that's my best part! (Or, my best quality!)
★ Why, thank you! I didn't think you had noticed!
★ Are you still hung up about that?
★ You know, I really couldn't care less what you think.
★ Hey, you're above that.
★ Hey, I was just starting to like you! Why use names like that?
★ I have a right to be a klutz! Geez, give a guy a chance!
★ Give me a break! Who said I was perfect?

Discussion Guidelines:

Essentially, people who are different get teased. If a martian walked into the room tomorrow, someone would make fun of his hair, his eyes, his speech, his movements. Unfortunately, humiliating other people about their differences makes us feel "one up" on them.

Kids who are different are going to be teased, so the gifted kids will probably qualify on several counts. Tell students that some teasing may be inevitable, but that doesn't make the substance of the remarks necessarily true. In the gifted students' case, their differences don't necessarily make them "weird," "a snot," "a ninety-pound weakling," "a nerd," or "Miss Perfect." It just means he or she is different, and certain people feel powerful when ridiculing them about it. When the teasing contains a grain of truth in it, sometimes the best tactic is to agree to and exaggerate it, as some of the examples above did. ("Geez, I'm so dense you'd need a pick ax to get this math stuff through.")

Teasing at its worst is not a particularly pleasant human trait. But it is human, and we have all dished it out at some time as well been the brunt of it. Some forms of teasing are also more tolerable than others, and we enjoy people we can kid around with and who understand our jokes are meant in fun. For gifted kids, however, the issues may be too sensitive to withstand remarks even when meant in fun. As the gifted kid relaxes about her or his differences, and learns to see the light side of things, the teasing will lessen. As a teacher, you can provide healthy examples of laughing at your own mistakes or idiosyncrasies, but stopping short of playing the clown.

Conclude the discussion by asking students to generate some ground rules about teasing they'd like to have for the classroom.

6. We feel overwhelmed by the number of things we can do in life.

Purpose: To examine specific choices facing students; to discuss the problems of pursuing one endeavor or interest.

Strategy: An individual task followed by group discussion.

Procedure: Writing the student's own obituary

Instructions to students: "You have twenty minutes to write your own obituary. Presume that you have had a long and full life and opportunities to accomplish much of what you'd like to do. Your obituary should contain facts (such as your schooling, your occupation, residence, whether you married or had children) as well as major accomplishments. Be sure to include personal characteristics, such as: "A shy and private woman, she is best remembered for her terrific creativity, and her love of chocolate and cats."

Discussion Questions:

1. Could we have a few volunteers read their obituaries, please?

2. What did you think about as you wrote this?

3. How did you arrive at these projections?

4. Did you have to make choices (between career options or accomplishments), or did you include everything you'd like to do?

5. How did you make these choices? How did you determine what was important?

6. Is it hard to make choices? Why or why not?

7. How possible do you suppose it is to have the life you've described?

8. What do you suppose you'd have to do to have this life?

Discussion Guidelines:

Explain to students that the purpose of the exercise is to help them focus on what is *most* important to them in life. Looking at this "after the fact," from the perspective of the obituary, does this quite neatly. For here one has to determine: How do I want to be remembered? What are my ambitions? What do I expect to accomplish? What is most meaningful to me—research awards, job titles, books published, community or social service, money acquired, family? Will I be remembered for my generosity to non-profit causes, leadership in the black community, or avid dedication to duck hunting? Will I have some notable defeats as well as successes? ("She lost her second bid for the senate but won the race for governor." "After a mountain climbing accident he didn't perform for another ten years; when he did it was to a sell-out crowd.") Will I have a family? Will I have more than one career? Will I have several major interests? Will I lead a life of obscurity or notoriety?

During the discussion, try to have students articulate why they made the projections they did, what choices they saw for themselves. Did they have to decide whether their final interest would lie in playing the piano or conducting? Between choreographing or dancing? Between teaching or raising children? Between medical research or practice? What kinds of personal values came into play with their decision-making?

Depending on the students' age, you may want to discuss what kinds of investments (time, energy, money) need to be made to pursue particular careers and the kind of training involved. Although the career counselor can help older students with these specifics, you might start kids thinking about their human and financial limitations. Emphasize also, however, that lifetimes are long, and opportunities to change course are ample.

Conclude by saying that, in general, having too many options before you is preferable to having too few. Having little or no choice in one's life is confining and stressful.

Flexibility is one of the best "problems" in life to have. The difficulty with too many options seems to stem from feeling that:

a) You have to choose too soon what you want to do;

b) It's hard to isolate or concentrate on one option—they all seem related and equally valid;

c) You can't decide which option will be better in the long run; or

d) You want to do it all—you don't want to give up or let go of one part of it.

Discuss these options with the students, and see what ramifications come with taking each option. What happens if you decide on a career too early? Too late? What happens if you try to do it all? What happens if you choose the wrong option? You can relieve their anxiety by telling them they have time to make up their minds, their decisions can be changed, that they may not be able to "do it all" all at once, but they may be able to do a lot of it spread out over their entire life. Reinforce the notion that choices have to be made; life will force you to make them. Yet choosing among alternatives is basically healthy; the action helps you channel energy into an area long enough to succeed in it.

For an interesting variation to this exercise, ask students to write an obituary for someone else in the class (make sure everyone has a partner, however). As long as known enemies are not paired, students may learn something constructive about how other people perceive them.

7. We feel different, alienated.

Purpose: To feel more comfortable with being different.

Strategy: Guest speaker (role model) and group discussion.

Procedure: Locate a former student from the gifted program or an adult in the community who has been identified as gifted and ask them to speak to the class. Ask them to address particular questions pertaining to peers, problems with isolation, connecting with a profession or avocation, and fitting in socially. You'll want them to talk about the rest of their life as well, but make sure they understand you're looking for an adult role model who can talk about the pains of isolation and growing up "so differently" from other kids. Have students prepare for this speaker by writing down questions in advance.

Suggested questions for the speaker:

1. Can you talk about your current profession or avocation, interests?

2. How did you figure out what you wanted to do? When did you become involved with . . .?

3. Can you talk about some of your experiences growing up? What was it like for you at your school(s)?

4. Were you in any special program(s)? Did you receive any special instruction?

5. How were you different from other kids? How were you similar?

6. Who were your friends? Were friendships a problem?

7. How did you get along with your siblings and parents?

8. It's been said by some gifted students that being gifted is something that doesn't "pay off" until you're grown up; as a kid you're only penalized for it. Is that true in your case? How can we help kids realize the benefits of being different at a young age?

9. What other advice for gifted kids do you have?

Facilitate group discussion between your guest speaker and kids after the speaker's prepared discussion is over. Perhaps the speaker could brainstorm, with you and the students, on ways we could all better appreciate differences among people.

Advice From Former Prodigies

"I would tell these children to relax and just try to enjoy what they are doing. Don't be compelled to be somebody they are not. Realize that you can be very talented in one area and just normal in others. One can get very enamored of the whole trip of being a prodigy. Also, you have to be disciplined . . . it's easy to become lazy if everything comes easy to you. But if kids do not have the motivation in themselves, I don't think someone else should force it on them.

"One more thing about this whole concept of being a prodigy. It's not where you start but where you level off that counts. I've gotten places faster than others, but the important thing, I think, is where I'm going to finally end up, and ultimately what my life's accomplishment is going to be. Many prodigies have gone on to lead very useful but certainly not spectacular lives. No one should be considered a failure if they were a prodigy when they were young and turn out to be good, solid, competent persons."

–George Barany, 1985[2]
Mpls/St. Paul Magazine

"Intelligence can be a trap. It can lead a young person to expect that success will come easily. It almost never does .... In the real world outside of school, drive, persistence, hard work, task commitment, and a little bit of luck count as much or more than intellect.

"What did happen to the Quiz Kids? Did we live up to our promise? Well, there's one Nobel prize-winner, James Watson, co-discoverer of the structure of DNA, but on the whole, we Quiz Kids are not as outstanding as in our youth. Some have done well, some not so well; we performed no better than others less gifted.

"If I were to boil down my message [to gifted kids] to two words, they would be, 'Be yourself.' "

–Ruth Duskin Feldman, 1985[3]
The Promise and Pain of Growing Up Gifted

---

8. We worry about world problems and feel helpless to do anything about them.

Purpose: To discuss students' feelings about world problems and generate possible ways to respond to these problems.

Strategy: General group discussion in which students voice their concerns and questions, and decide the limits of their responsibility. Then, the group brainstorms possible courses of action on one or two of the most commonly shared concerns.

Discussion Questions:

1. Today we're going to talk about how affected we feel by certain world problems. It's been said that advanced technology, like television, and satellite communications, is bringing

the world closer together—we're becoming a "family of man" in a "global village" (McCluhan). Although this may be good in some ways, it certainly makes us more aware of how stressful life can be. Violence from around the world comes into our living rooms via TV, radio, and newspapers. On the other hand, by exposing conflicts to many world nations simultaneously, the media may be helping to contain violence. Are there any world problems you feel especially concerned about?

2. How have you learned about this issue—from parents? School? The media? What do these sources have to say about it?

3. Is this a confusing issue for you? Do you understand why it's a problem (why people in Central America are fighting; why people are demonstrating against nuclear energy; why terrorism is directed at the United States)?

4. Would you like to get more information on this subject? Where or how do you suppose you could get it?

5. Do people at home or in this room have strong feelings about this topic? What are they?

6. Are there any other social problems, perhaps closer to home (i.e., neighborhood, city) that concern you?

   (Repeat questions 2–5 for this and other concerns.)

7. Okay, now we've talked about the kinds of problems that worry us, and some specific questions we have about these problems. Let's take one of these concerns and brainstorm what you, individually or in a group, could do about it. (List on board and discuss.)

Discussion Guidelines:

In leading this discussion be prepared for two kinds of problems. One is the student who is so overly sensitive to world problems, particularly suffering and violence, that she can't separate herself from the problems and feels overly responsible for them. It is very hard to accept millions of people starving in Nigeria, and the threat of nuclear holocaust. But a student shouldn't feel the suffering of others to the extent it immobilizes her, or feel such extreme anxiety for the future when the future is yet to be. Rather than working to increase the sensitivity of this student, relieve her of guilt feelings and help her put the situation in a place separate from herself. Invite her to learn more about the issues (both positive and negative aspects) and to take constructive social action. But remind her also that *she* is healthy and safe; has time to grow up and deal with these problems as an adult; and is not expected to take them on single-handedly now. Empirical evidence shows the world will probably continue to turn, despite the most terrible events.

The second kind of problem concerns the opposite kind of student, one who is apathetic and lacks sensitivity towards people suffering in remote places in circumstances he can't relate to. This student is probably uncomfortable discussing world problems. He doesn't want them to concern him, and therefore believes they don't. (Or, he believes the government or some superpower is controlling things, which means—for better or worse—it's out of his hands, he can't do anything about it.)

For this student, you may want to emphasize how important individual efforts can be. Ask students whether they can think of a time when the collective efforts of many people changed the course of history (or life in their city district, school, or family). Emphasize how basically similar all human beings are in terms of needs and wants, regardless of their nationality or status. Ask students to join in a discussion about what the proper level of responsibility for others is— how important it is to care about other people even when their troubles don't involve us directly.

Depending on the kinds of opinions expressed and the types of students in your classroom, you may want to turn the discussion into a spontaneous debate. Or, ask students to debate the issues and their chosen course of action at a later date.

Another kind of issue that may come up during discussion is that of accepting or rejecting adults' belief systems. Students are in the process of developing their own beliefs and values—about abortion, marriage, politics, religion, and nuclear armament. They may be particularly eager to talk about how their views differ from those of their parents, or how influenced they have been by a socially conscious parent.

In conclusion, help students understand there is much to sorrow for in the world, but much to rejoice over as well. We all need to "work for a better world," and every effort counts. Clarify whatever misconceptions of theirs you discover. (In one discussion of nuclear war, it was discovered students thought there were hundreds of "buttons" all over the world that anyone could push to blow up the planet, at any time.) Bring unrealistic fears back down to the ground. Encourage them to take action on social issues because it is morally good, and working for change can make one feel more positive. But dissuade them from feeling overly responsible (particularly as the "gifted youth of tomorrow") for saving the world.

You may want to work through the year building your list of possible actions to take in assuming social responsibility. Options such as letter-writing, newsletter- or article-writing, neighborhood organizations, fact-finding tours, individual recycling habits, demonstrations, forming committees, joining national organizations, sending private donations, and volunteer work can highlight how many individual and collective activities can be pursued.

Notes

1. Ronald T. Zaffrann and Nick Colangelo, "Counseling With Gifted and Talented Students," *Gifted Child Quarterly* 21(3):313.

2. Steve Kaplan, "Junior Achievers," *Mpls/St. Paul Magazine* (June, 1985):57.

3. Ruth Duskin Feldman, "The Promise and Pain of Growing Up Gifted," *Gifted/Creative/Talented* (May/June, 1985):1.

7

STRATEGIES: ONGOING GROUP SUPPORT

As you probably already realize, supporting the emotional and social growth of human beings lies at the heart of affective education. The humanistic movement of the last two decades has dedicated itself to helping students learn more about themselves and about their relations with other people. In the following "proposal" educator/author Larry Chase offers a nice summary of affective education:[1]

> What I am suggesting here is that we do for social and emotional growth what we have done so well with reading. What this country needs is not a "Right to Read" program but a "Right to Feel Good About Yourself" program. Imagine what would happen if the government made that kind of commitment! By 1980 every public school would have a program designed to teach children how to understand themselves and others and how to make decisions, set goals, like themselves, cope with normal problems, clarify values and accomplish all the other objectives contained in the board of education's philosophy, including an understanding of their rights and obligations as human beings and as citizens.

The following compilation of strategies owes much to the humanistic psychology and education movements generally, and to Sidney Simon and his colleagues, Jack Canfield, Harold Wells, and Larry Chase specifically. Affective education is certainly applicable to every student and every classroom, but we feel this selection covers some of the best and most fundamental exercises applicable to gifted kids.

The strategies are presented under two headings: values clarification and assertiveness training. Values clarification helps students define who they are and what they value, thus building self-knowledge or intrapersonal intelligence. Assertiveness training focuses on group skills and behaviors, thus building knowledge of self-among-others or interpersonal knowledge.

As with the exercises listed previously, a key to building trust within the group is to begin with the least threatening exercises and proceed to those calling for more self-disclosure.

VALUES CLARIFICATION

1. Unfinished Sentences

Purpose: To have students identify dreams and wishes, likes, dislikes, habits, opinions, and customs, etc., without having to explain or defend them; to see the range of differences between people; to get to know other students.

Strategy: Circle discussion in which first the teacher, then other students, throw out an unfinished statement which everyone has a chance to complete.

Sample Sentences:

1. The best time to watch TV is . . .

2. If I could live anywhere in the world, I'd live . . .

3. If I could be any animal I'd be a . . .

4. If I could be any famous person I'd be . . .

5. At 7:00 a.m. on Monday mornings my temperament can best be described as . . .

6. My strongest political opinion concerns . . .

7. The style of dress I admire most is worn by . . .

8. The chore I mind doing the least around the house is . . .

9. My favorite holiday is . . .

10. I get silly (or angry, or excited) when . . .

11. I would like it if in this class we . . .

12. My favorite childhood game was . . .

Discussion Guidelines:

After you go around the circle several times, ask the students if they have any unfinished sentences they'd like others to answer. List their suggestions on the board and vote on which the class should try. (You may need to remind them that because students have the right to pass on any question, if the suggested sentence stems are inappropriate, not many people will want to answer it.)

(This exercise is based on a strategy written by Simon, Howe, and Kirschenbaum in *Values Clarification.*[2])

2. Role Models

Purpose: To have students identify their ideal role model as well as their most despised role model; to analyze these models' traits and characteristics.

Strategy: Independent writing and group discussion.

Procedure: After introducing students to the topic, you'll be asking several questions which students respond to by writing in their private journals. (It doesn't have to be recorded in a journal, but the writing is not to be handed in.) After the written portion is completed, the class discusses how they approached the questions.

Questions for the Written Portion

Instructions to students: Today we're going to do some writing and talking about role models—about heroes and anti-heroes. These can be either actual or imaginary people that we admire and emulate, as well as people we dislike and try to be different from. Please find your journal (or piece of paper) and take a moment to clear your mind of other thoughts. I'm going to ask you to close your eyes and think about a series of questions. After each question you'll have several minutes to write down your thoughts in whatever fashion you choose.

1. Who in the world would you like most to be like? This person can be real or imaginary, dead or alive, famous or ordinary, known personally by you or not. When you've thought about a range of possibilities, write down this person's name if real (e.g., Barbra Streisand) or role if imaginary (e.g., world-famous scientist).

2. What is this person like? Name as many characteristics as you can, including age, appearance, national origin, intellectual and other personal qualities. What does this person have (e.g., material goods, prestige, awards)? What does this person do?

3. What about this person is most desirable?

4. Now I want you to think about the opposite. Who in the world would you most hate to be? This can also be a real or imaginary person, dead or alive, famous or ordinary, known personally by you or not. When you've thought about a range of possibilities, write down this person's name or role.

5. What is this person like? Name as many attributes as you can. What does this person have? What does this person do?

6. What about this person is most undesirable?

7. Which person do you resemble most, the desired role model or the undesired role model? How? Explain as thoroughly as you can how you are similar and different from these models.

Discussion Questions:

1. Would anyone care to share their ideal role models with us? Who did you name?

2. Have you admired this person for some time now, or did you identify him or her just today?

3. Under "most desirable characteristics," how many of you listed wealth, fame, possessions like cars, symbols of power? (Ask for a show of hands.) How many of you listed beauty or physical strength? How many of you listed abstract personal qualities such as loyalty, good humor, honesty? How many of you listed talents such as creativity, intelligence, painting, music, leadership?

4. What were some of the most undesirable characteristics you identified in negative role models?

5. Can role models change? Will this one last your whole life?

6. How "true to life" is your current role model? Do you suppose your ideal model is actually the way you perceive him or her, all the time?

7. Can you see—or hypothesize—some human faults in your ideal role model? What are they?

8. Is it good to have positive and negative role models?

Discussion Guidelines:

Many times the images we carry around of ideal people are one-dimensional or false. We only see the flattering aspects of our heroes, only the grand benefits of their achievements. As adults, of course, we learn that even outstanding people have personal faults, the most famous of lives have their challenges and disappointments, the "coolest" guy around, his moments of vulnerability. Assuredly, whatever role in life we ultimately play will combine both pleasant and unpleasant features.

Students may enjoy keeping records of who their role models are and how they change over time. Some may even be interested in developing an ideal character (fleshed out with human traits such as competitiveness or impatience, or a tendency to overeat) as an imaginary model to emulate. (Should the character's faults reflect the limitations the students see in themselves and can't change easily?)

To elaborate further on this exercise, bring in character descriptions from your favorite novels or current classroom texts. Include "pulp" novels, love stories, serious fiction, history books, classics, *People* magazine, and others. Either post them weekly on the board, reading aloud during a two-minute break, or discuss them at length as a follow-up to this exercise. Notice how flat or stereotypic the characters are drawn in dime novels (all-good, all-beautiful, all-evil, all-suffering), and how much more rounded or human they are in critically acclaimed work.

3. Dear Abby

Purpose: To have students discuss situations in which personal values and ethics come into play; to problem-solve and make judgments based on these values.

Preparation: Collect Dear Abby and Ann Landers columns, or write fictitious letters that illustrate particular conflicts you want students to discuss (see samples below).

Strategy: Divide up into small groups and circulate the letters. Groups are to read the same two or three letters, discuss the issues, and compose a response. When the groups are finished, reassemble into a large group and have them read aloud and compare their responses.

Sample Letters

Dear Abby;

I have a younger brother who is a real pain. He's also not very bright. My mother and dad are always on my case, trying to get me (the math honors student) to help him do his homework. If the dope were a little more appreciative I might do it, but otherwise, what's in it for me? Do you think I should have to help him?

Signed, My Brother's Keeper

Dear Ann,

I feel really confused. Last week a guy I'm interested in asked me out. I said sure, I'd like to go. Then he called yesterday to say the date was off. Suddenly he was "busy." My friend Sally thinks he changed his mind because he saw my grade-point average and SAT scores (they were published in the school newspaper; I guess they're pretty good). Apparently, he told a friend standing next to him, "Oh, no, not another brain!"

How can I convince him I'm not "just a brain"?

Signed, More Than Mental Activity

Dear Abby;

I have been into drugs for several years, but not so it causes me any problems. My parents and teachers don't suspect a thing because I still get my work in on time and do my thing. You probably don't approve, but anyone who is anyone in the music business knows that drugs are cool if you know what you're doing.

The problem is that I have a friend who's getting into the really hard stuff, mixing it with liquor and other pills, and doesn't know when to stop. I tell him he's going to burn out real fast, do a Belushi you might say, but he laughs it off and then manages to get me too wasted to argue.

I think he needs help but I'm scared to turn him in on account of other people suspecting me of being involved and a bad influence (this kid is younger than me and lives in my neighborhood). Plus my parents would kill me if they ever found out, and my brothers in the band wouldn't speak to me again. What should I do? I'm really worried about this kid.

Signed, Bad in Baltimore

4. Values Grid

Purpose: To see how strongly we value certain positions or actions, and how strongly we assert these values.

Preparation: Prepare a values grid handout similar to the one drawn below. There should be room for approximately five to seven concerns, and columns labeled 1, 2, 3, 4, 5, 6, 7. Explanations for the column headings should be provided, as in our example.

Strategy: Individual rating activity, plus small group discussion.

Procedure: Ask students to recall some of the world problems or social issues they discussed in one of the previous exercises (see Chapter Six, Feeling Overwhelmed by World Problems). Ask them to list a few of these or other concerns on their values grid, and explain the headings. After the students have rated each concern, have them meet in groups of three or four to discuss why they rated each issue at each particular level.

CONCERN	1	2	3	4	5	6	7
1.							
2.							
3.							
4.							
5.							
ETC.							

(The seven levels (or "subprocesses") of valuing are based on the work of Louis Rath, Harmin Merrill, and Sidney Simon in *Values and Teaching*, Charles E. Merrill, Columbus, Ohio; 1966.)

People hold different opinions and values to different degrees. Some issues we care about terrifically, others not so much. The seven levels can be defined as:

1) Prizing and cherishing, 2) Publicly affirming, when appropriate, 3) Choosing from alternatives, 4) Choosing after consideration of consequences, 5) Choosing freely, 6) Acting, and 7) Acting with a pattern, consistency.

Instructions to Students: Consider how strongly you feel about the issues listed on your values grid. Rate each of them from one to seven by asking yourself the questions:

1. Am I proud of my position? (Do I prize or cherish this value?)

2. Have I publicly affirmed my position?

3. Have I chosen my position from alternatives?

4. Have I chosen my position after considering the consequences?

5. Have I chosen my position freely?

6. Have I acted on or done anything about my beliefs?

7. Have I acted with repetition, pattern, or consistency on this issue?

Discussion Guidelines:

The purpose of the discussion is not to debate the issues but to determine how strongly the issues are felt. Students may realize, for example, that they care about something, but mostly because they are influenced by a parent's or best friend's involvement. They may discover that they care tremendously about an issue, but have done nothing to affirm it or act upon it.

Discuss with students how convictions evolve over time. It may be many years before they can publicly affirm some of their strongest beliefs. Or, they may already be on their way to discovering that affirmation is possible and rewarding.

(This exercise is based on a strategy written by Simon, Howe, and Kirschenbaum in *Values Clarification.*[2])

5. Where Am I Going?

Purpose: To have students take stock of where they've been, where they are, and where they are going.

Strategy: Student interviews (done in pairs).

Procedure: Students are assigned partners and given an interview protocol (see below). The students have fifteen minutes or so to interview their partner and record their answers. When they're finished, students exchange papers (each partner keeps a copy of his or her own answers).

Handout: Interview Protocol

To the interviewer: Feel free to improvise on the questions below. A good interviewer keeps his partner talking by listening and asking follow-up questions! Make sure you record as much of your partner's answers as possible.

The Past

1. Tell me a brief history of your life.
2. What five adjectives would you choose to describe your past life?
3. What's the earliest memory you have?
4. Which years have been rocky or difficult, which ones smooth? Why?

The Present

5. How are things today different or similar from your past?
6. Have you changed from two years ago? How? Why?
7. What kind of person are you now?
8. How do you feel today?
9. Are you getting what you want out of life? Why or why not?

The Future

10. What do you see happening to you in the next four years?
11. How would you like to grow or change?
12. What's the worst thing that could happen?
13. What can you do to get what you want out of life?
14. What's preventing you from doing it?

Activity Guidelines:

If students are unused to interviewing, you may want to precede this exercise with some simple communication skill exercises in which partners practice active listening, rephrasing, and affirmative responses.

ASSERTIVENESS TRAINING

1. Defining Assertive, Non-assertive, and Aggressive Behavior

Purpose: To understand these behavioral concepts.

Strategy: Two handouts plus group discussion.

Preparation: Prepare one handout in which the definitions, goals, and basic messages of assertive, non-assertive, and aggressive behavior are outlined. Use the one shown below or modify it with your own interpretations.
Prepare a second handout in which the "reasons"

and consequences of assertive, non-assertive and aggressive behavior are listed.

Assertive Behavior

Definition:	Goals:	Basic Messages:
Assertiveness is any behavior that indicates a person is standing up for his or her rights; is able to express honest feelings comfortably in a direct and straightforward manner without denying the rights of others or feeling undue anxiety or guilt.	The goals of assertiveness include conflict resolution and communication; getting basic needs met; earning respect and respecting others; seeing that justice prevails and no rights are violated.	The basic messages behind assertive behaviors are: I count; you count. This is what I think; this is what I feel. This is what I want and need. This is how I see the situation. I realize my thoughts and needs are different than yours; both sets of perception are valid.

Non-assertive Behavior

Definition:	Goals:	Basic Messages:
Behavior that negates one's personal worth or rights by failing to express feelings, thoughts, or needs honestly, or expressing them in such an apologetic, self-demeaning manner they can easily be disregarded.	To appease others and to avoid conflict at all costs; to avoid visibility or responsibility; to "make people like me."	I don't count; only you count. You can take advantage of me. My thoughts and feelings don't matter; only yours do. I don't want to be held accountable.

Aggressive Behavior

Definition:	Goals:	Basic Messages:
Behavior that asserts personal rights and expresses thoughts, feelings, and needs in a manner which violates or negates the rights or feelings of others. Behavior that is degrading, humiliating, belittling, or overpowering.	To dominate and to win; to force other people to give in or lose.	I count; you don't count. My thoughts and feelings are important; yours aren't.

Discussion Questions:

After giving students the first handout to read, go through the definitions, goals, and basic messages of each type of behavior, asking students for examples as you go along. After students appear to understand the terms and concepts, and you have a fair number of examples of assertive, non-assertive, and aggressive behavior, have students discuss the following questions and list their responses on the board:

1. **Why do people act non-assertively?**
2. **What happens when someone is consistently non-assertive? What are the consequences?**
3. **Why do people act aggressively?**
4. **What happens when someone is consistently aggressive? What are the consequences?**
5. **Why do people act assertively?**
6. **What happens to people who are consistently assertive? What are some of the possible consequences?**

Discussion Guidelines:

Readers take note that the "reasons" for certain behaviors are the explanations that people provide (for themselves or others) for their actions; we're not talking about deep psychological causes.

Help students think through reasons why they or other people are assertive/non-assertive/aggressive by recalling some of their earlier examples. Situations which may call for assertiveness include: confronting a teacher on a bad mark, or for keeping them from taking an advanced course; teasing from other kids; backhanded "compliments" about being gifted from adults or peers.

Be especially sensitive to the responses of your female students. Women are still greatly conditioned to behave in non-assertive ways; they are expected to please other people, settle disputes, avoid conflict. They are most praised for being agreeable, compliant, and selfless. Sometimes they are taught to fear the spotlight, or to feel guilty when their talents put them there. As an insightful counselor's guide entitled "The Gifted Girl: Helping Her Be the Best She Can Be"[3] states, girls often devalue their efforts and abilities as a result. Either they deny success, or attribute it to luck or exceptional effort (not ability).

Then, distribute and discuss a second handout, which is prepared in the fashion below:

Reasons for Non-assertive Behavior

1. Fear of losing other peoples' approval, friendship

2. Desire to avoid conflict at any cost

3. Fear of responsibility, expectations

4. Need to maintain low profile, image of unimportance

5. Mistaking assertion for aggression, and non-assertion for politeness

6. Fits in with value system of being "good," or of being "feminine"

7. To win praise from other people for being selfless, agreeable, "nice"

Consequences of Non-assertive Behavior

1. Personal integrity gets sacrificed

2. It's difficult to maintain close, non-exploitative relationships

3. Internal tension and stress can cause somatic illnesses and depression

4. Other people lose respect and withdraw from you

5. Feelings of insecurity, loneliness, and resentment may cause failure on the job or in other professional or personal endeavors

Reasons for Acting Aggressively

1. Fear of becoming "weak," of losing control

2. Need to dominate over others, win at all costs

3. Need to feel or seem powerful

4. Maintain image of perfection by making sure others can't confront you on your mistakes

5. Can't accept other people's right to have rights

6. Responding inappropriately after having behaved non-assertively for much of one's life

7. Over-reaction to past emotional experiences

Consequences of Aggressive Behavior

1. Other people lose their respect and withdraw from you

2. Other people retaliate, directly or indirectly

3. Failure to establish close relationships

4. Failure to succeed on the job

5. Feelings of guilt, shame, embarrassment, loneliness

6. Internal stress, somatic illnesses

7. May lead to future non-assertiveness

Reasons for Acting Assertively

1. Increases one's self-respect, self-control, self-confidence
2. Reduces need for approval from or dependence on others
3. Usually increases respect and admiration of others
4. Reduces insecurity and vulnerability
5. Closer, more satisfying relationships result
6. Reduces stress and minimizes chances for somatic illness
7. Maximizes possibility of both parties achieving goal and meeting needs

Possible Consequences of Assertive Behavior

1. Other people may misunderstand and be angry
2. May lose old friends, have to find new ones
3. New behaviors may feel uncomfortable at first
4. New opportunities, new goals, new directions
5. Happiness, satisfaction with relationships and one's life
6. New feelings of security and generosity

Advise students to take the handouts home and think about their own behaviors and the behaviors of others. A possible assignment is to have them write down, for next time, three incidences in which they either witness each type of behavior, or find themselves responding assertively, non-assertively, and aggressively. This can be followed by the next exercise.

2. Role-Playing Assertive, Non-assertive, and Aggressive Behavior

Purpose: To experience assertive, non-assertive, and aggressive behaviors and associated feelings.

Strategy: Small group discussion and role play.

Procedure: Review the definitions of assertive, aggressive, and non-assertive behaviors and ask the class whether they "collected" any examples of such behaviors in the intervening week. Ask students to relate their observations. Then divide the class into small groups and introduce the role play exercise.

Preparation: The role play will involve scenarios of possible conflict. If possible, pick up and use some of the situations observed by students, but be prepared with at least three "trying situations" which could prompt either assertive, non-assertive, or aggressive behavior. Here are three possible vignettes to describe orally or prepare on a handout:

A. A group of students is discussing whether girls are "any good" at sports. Most of the students talking are male, and they're laughing about several female athletes in the school who are "built like a guy" and would be "good for nothing" on a date. Do you decide to say something? What do you say?

B. During class elections you see that a popular but not very competent (in your opinion) student has been nominated for class president. A lot of his friends are endorsing him, even though the obvious choice for this role is another student, who is exceptionally well qualified. Nominations are about to close and the opportunity to discuss the candidates is almost over. Do you decide to say something? What do you say?

C. Tests are being handed back in math class and the scores are clearly marked at the top of each paper. The teacher calls off the names of the highest scoring students first, and yours heads the list. Several students snicker: "Can't you do anything wrong?"

"Of course she gets 100s, what else does she do except study? She's too ugly to date," and other, similar comments. Do you decide to say something? What do you say?

Instructions to Small Groups for the Role-Play

You have ten minutes to prepare for a role-play. As a group, choose one of the vignettes I've just presented, or select one of the situations you observed this past week and develop your own scenario. Select roles for yourselves, develop your character (assertive, non-assertive, or aggressive), and generate possible responses. Don't rehearse the actual role-play ahead of time, just prepare for it.

Discussion Questions:

After the group presents its role-play, ask the students:

1. What kind of behavior were you acting out? Aggressive, assertive, or non-assertive?

2. How did it feel to act that way?

3. How did it feel to have the other student(s) respond with . . . (either aggressive, assertive, or non-assertive behavior)?

4. Can we reverse the roles, and have you try this role . . . ?

5. Can you do the role-play again, this time responding with a different kind of behavior?

Discussion Guidelines:

Focus on the feelings students experience as they assume the different postures of assertiveness, non-assertiveness, and aggressiveness. Clarify any misconceptions they have about the nature of assertiveness.

3. Practicing Assertiveness

Purpose: To have students practice simple assertive statements.

Strategy: Group discussion on how assertive people communicate (e.g., eye contact, voice control, physical stance, calm appearance, "I" messages) and role-play.

Handout: Use the following as a handout or as a guide for your discussion.

How Do Assertive People Communicate?

1. They make "I" statements.

They make statements which reflect their own thoughts and feelings, rather than blame others, or hold others responsible for them. Examples:

Instead of This . . .	*They Say . . .*
"You make me so mad" . . .	"I'm really angry"
"If only you"	"When you do this . . . I feel . . ."
"You should"	"I want . . ."
"You never"	"I would like it if you . . ."

2. *They can talk about themselves* and their achievements candidly with other people. If they do something interesting or something they feel good about, they can talk about it with others.

3. *They can talk about their feelings.* They can express their likes and dislikes openly and spontaneously. They can say, "I really like that person," or "I'm really nervous about that."

4. *They accept compliments* graciously and with pleasure, saying "Thank you," or "I'm pleased with this myself." They do not punish the complimenter by responding, "Oh,

that old thing," or "It's not good enough," or "I didn't really do much."

5. *They make greeting talk.* They smile and look people in the eye, saying "Hello, nice to see you," rather than mumbling, nodding silently, or looking embarrassed.

6. *They use appropriate body gestures.* Their facial expressions, voice inflections, and body posture are relaxed and convey the same feelings as their words. They are not agitated, restless, but calm and focused.

7. *They ask for clarification.* If someone gives them directions or explanations that are not clear, they ask to have them repeated or clarified. Rather than going away feeling confused and dumb, they say, "I didn't understand that. Would you please repeat it?"

8. *They ask why.* When they are asked to do something they don't understand, or something that seems unreasonable, they ask, "Why do you want me to do this?" or "Does it have to be done this way?"

9. *They can say "no."* They do not let themselves be talked into doing things they do not want to do. They say "no" to requests without feeling guilty. They don't have to always go along with what the group wants to do.

10. *They ask others for help.* They ask others to do things, listen to them, assist them. They do this without feeling guilty, and with the understanding that the other persons have the right to say "no."

11. *They are persistent* without being obnoxious. If they have a legitimate complaint, request, or opinion they can continue to restate it despite resistance from the other party. They do not give in prematurely, and they do not accept the other party as automatically right. Neither do they attempt to humiliate or negate the other person's feelings or thoughts.

Discussion Questions:

Review the handout or elicit these characteristics on the board. When the students seem clear about the listed behaviors, have them practice several simple assertive behaviors. **For example:**

1. Have students pair off and practice walking up, shaking hands, smiling, looking the other person in the eye, and saying, "Hello. My name is——. I'm glad to see you."

2. In their same pairs, have students sit across from one another and deliver one "I" message. This message should state how the speaker is feeling or what she is thinking about a real or imaginary issue and is to be delivered face-to-face with full eye contact.

3. In groups of four, have each student take a turn addressing the group with a request. The statement should take the form of "I need" or "I want."

4. If the group has reached a good level of trust, ask each student to stand up in the class and name one achievement or quality they are particularly proud of.

5. Finally, tell the students you are going to go around the room asking them individually to do something. They are to say "no" to your request if it seems unreasonable, "yes" if it seems reasonable, and ask questions if they need clarification.

Some sample messages:

☆ Susan, would you please prepare that book review to present to the class by tomorrow?

☆ Harry, when you're done playing Dungeons and Dragons in here will you please turn off the lights?

☆ George, will you tell us something about last night's homework?

☆ Genevieve, could you use your free time today to help Tommy rewrite his paper?

Discussion Guidelines:

Follow up the practice sessions listed for the first four behaviors above by asking students to describe how they felt acting assertively, and how they feel now. Ask them if this gives them any ideas for pursuing chronic problems at home or school.

Allowing students to confront you, as in the last practice example, can be a really fun way to strengthen students' convictions in themselves. Your challenges can be silly as well as true-to-life. They should be quick requests; no further answers besides "yes," "no," or "can you explain that again, please?" are required of students, and no punishments are attached! The point is simply to allow them the experience of thinking through the legitimacy of requests and responding assertively.

4. Resent-Need-Appreciate

Purpose: To help students learn to express difficult feelings such as resentment, needs, and appreciation.

Strategy: A ten-minute written exercise, followed by small group discussion.

Instructions to students for the written exercise: Take out a sheet of paper and list along the left-hand side the names of four important people in your life. (The names should be spaced far apart vertically.) One of the people must be in this classroom. The others may include family, friends, or anyone with whom you have a personal relationship. (You may not choose a rock star or famous person!) Then make three long vertical columns to the right of the names. At the top of the columns list these separate headings: Resent, Need, Appreciate.

For each of the names listed, write down one sentence under each of the headings. Write: "I resent you for . . ." "I need you to . . ." "I do appreciate how (or, that) you . . ." For each person, you must think back and

144

find one thing they do that bothers you and causes resentment, and uncover the real need behind that resentment. Turn that need into a statement of need or request, then try to find something about that person you also appreciate.

For example:

"I *resent* you for making me do all this work that I hate."

"I *need* to work on something more meaningful."

"But I do *appreciate* how much you taught me last semester."

Tell the students that resentments can build up between people when their values or attitudes conflict, or when some person's aggressive behavior has gone unchecked. And behind most resentments lie needs, either subconscious or unspoken. As with, "I resent your teasing. I need respect just as much as any other human being." The trick is to verbalize these feelings (at least to yourself), instead of saying, "You idiot! You make me sick you're so stupid."

Ask students why they think it is difficult for so many people to verbalize gratitude. Ask them to think hard about appreciating people for certain qualities or actions, even when there are other parts they dislike.

When students have finished their lists, divide them into small groups of about five. Students share their statements, and help brainstorm responses for any group members who were stumped.

Discussion Questions:

1. Was it difficult to think of resentments?

2. Is it okay to resent people? Is it always avoidable? How is it we resent the people we care about so deeply?

3. Were you able to figure out the need that lay beneath the resentment? Were you aware of this need before?

4. Is it bad to have this need? Do other people share that need?

5. If the resentment stems from a difference in values or opinions, can you discuss this openly?

6. Could you find something to appreciate about these people as well?

7. Would it be difficult to tell these people you resent/appreciate them? Why or why not?

Discussion Guidelines:

It can be quite illuminating to discover how deeply we resent someone or some actions. Realizations of this sort are liberating. Also illuminating is the discovery of the need—usually tied to a right—which has been "offended." By tracking down the cause of resentment we usually do discover (in Simon's, et al., view) a value or standard. This is valuable self-knowledge.

Your role here is to help kids backtrack these emotions, and practice expressing their feelings. You may want to end this, or other classes, by standing in a circle and asking everyone whether they have a resentment, need, or appreciation to share. An "appreciation" from you is, of course, always appreciated!

(This exercise is based on the work of Sidney Simon, Leland Howe, and Howard Kirschenbaum in *Values Clarification*[2]).

5. Brain Power

Purpose: To brainstorm how students can assert themselves positively when school seems boring and irrelevant.

Strategy: Brainstorming session, followed by task/action plans.

Procedure: Begin this exercise by reminding students of your previous exercise on boredom (Chapter Six). Ask them to recall the insights they gained as they studied the photographs. After setting the ground rules for brainstorming, ask them to name all the ways *they* could possibly make school more interesting, more relevant.

Discussion Guidelines:

An exciting way to close this exercise is to sketch out a plan of action for one or more of the ideas. This will depend on the type of suggestions your students generate. In one trial, students came up with both relatively simple steps (such as the testing-out of material in order to do an independent study), and complex plans (such as forming a committee of students, parents, and teachers to study the idea of implementing advanced placement classes at the school).

If the students become excited with a particular idea, help them think through a task/action plan. Essentially this is just a list of process steps, keyed to dates and assigned to people.

Notes

1. Larry Chase, *The Other Side of The Report Card* (Glenview, Illinois: 1975), p. 3.

2. Sidney Simon, Leland W. Howe, and Howard Kirschenbaum, *Values Clarification* (New York: A & W Publishers, Inc., 1972).

3. Linda B. Addison, *The Gifted Girl: Helping Her Be the Best She Can Be* (Bethesda, Maryland: The Equity Institute).

APPENDIX
Student Questionnaire*

Dear Students,

This questionnaire is about you—and I'd like you to fill it out so I can be a better teacher for this class. There are no "right" or "wrong" answers. The most important thing is to think honestly about the questions. You may remain anonymous if you wish, and choose to skip some questions. But try answering them all—you'll get more out of the exercise if you do. All answers will be kept strictly confidential, although we'll be talking about some of these questions later on as a group.

A. DEMOGRAPHICS

★ your age _____   ★ your gender _____ / _____
                                              M   F

★ number of years in a gifted program or class
  (please circle one): 0 1 2 3 4 5 6 or more

B. QUESTIONS YOU MAY ALREADY BE ASKING YOURSELF

1. What does gifted mean to you? _____
2. How do you feel about the label? _____
3. How were you selected for this class or program? _____
4. How do you feel about the selection process? _____
5. What do you think the purpose of this class/program is? (Check all that apply.)

_____ I don't know

_____ Harder work than other classes

_____ More work than other classes

_____ More challenging or interesting work

_____ Friendships with people like me

_____ Place to have fun

_____ Place where I'm not considered weird

_____ Learn something new

_____ Be stimulated to try new things

_____ Nothing different from other classes

_____ Other (write it down): _____

_____

C. FEELINGS ABOUT YOURSELF

6. In what ways are you the same as most other kids your age? What things do you have in common? _____

*Retype the questionnaire and leave generous amounts of space for write-in questions.

148

7. In what ways are you different from most other kids your age? What makes you unique? _____

---

8. In terms of popularity . . . (check *one*):
   _____ I have no close friends
   _____ I have one or two close friends
   _____ I have several (four or five) close friends
   _____ I have a lot of close friends
   _____ I have tons of close friends and am liked by most everybody

9. In terms of how you feel about yourself . . . (check *one*)
   _____ I hate myself
   _____ I don't like myself much
   _____ I like parts of myself, but dislike other parts
   _____ I feel okay about myself
   _____ Most of the time, I like myself a lot
   _____ I've always liked myself a whole lot

10. If there's one thing you'd like to change about yourself it would be:

---

11. The best thing about you, as far as you're concerned, is: _____

D. CONFLICTS

12. Indicate how often you experience the following feelings or problems by circling 1, 2, 3, 4, or 5 based on this scale: (1 = not at all; 2 = hardly ever; 3 = sometimes; 4 = alot; 5 = all the time)

Feeling or Problem	How Frequently Felt?
a. *I wonder what gifted means*	1 2 3 4 5
b. *I wonder why they say I'm gifted, and what is expected of me*	1 2 3 4 5
c. *School is too easy, boring*	1 2 3 4 5
d. *Parents, teachers, and friends expect me to be perfect all the time*	1 2 3 4 5
e. *Friends who really understand me are hard to find*	1 2 3 4 5
f. *Kids often tease me about being smart (or for being interested in certain things, getting high grades, etc.)*	1 2 3 4 5
g. *I feel overwhelmed by the number of things I can understand or do*	1 2 3 4 5
h. *I feel different, alienated, alone*	1 2 3 4 5
i. *I worry about world problems, or problems in my family, and feel helpless to do anything about these problems*	1 2 3 4 5

13. What's your biggest problem or difficulty in life right now? _____

---

14. Generally how do you feel about your life? (Make a slash somewhere along the continuum.) _____

|——|

Feel extremely bad, upset,   Feel really great,
worried; think about   confident, happy
dying

E. SUPPORT SYSTEMS

15. Who do you share your feelings or problems with when you're wondering what life is all about, or who you are? Who do you go to—or like to be around—when things aren't so great? (Check all that apply):

_____ friend

_____ mother

_____ father

_____ sister

_____ brother

_____ other relative

_____ pet (dog, cat)

_____ coach

_____ clergy

_____ school counselor

_____ camp counselor

_____ psychologist or doctor

_____ official Big Brother or Sister

_____ other grown-up (neighbor)

_____ teacher

_____ I prefer just being alone

_____ I don't think about that kind of stuff

16. What do you do to feel good about yourself? (Check all that apply):

_____ think or study harder

_____ get some exercise (get on my bike, go for a run, head for the gym, dance)

_____ call up a friend on the phone

_____ write in a journal

_____ paint or do other art-work or crafts

_____ play an instrument

_____ work on a project (club, play, newspaper)

_____ play harder in sports

_____ earn some extra money

_____ get outdoors and go somewhere (shopping, park)

_____ watch TV

_____ talk to my parents

_____ talk to my teacher

_____ listen to music

_____ eat

_____ use relaxation techniques (yoga, meditation)

_____ other (please write it down):

17. And finally, if you could get this class/program to do or provide ONE THING for you, it would be: _____

★ name (optional) _____

Teacher Inventory

1. Personally, I think gifted means . . . _____

2. I do / do not use this label because . . . _____

3. I identify with the gifted in the following ways: _____

4. I'm different than the gifted in the following ways: _____

5. When I tell other people that I work with gifted students, I feel (check all that apply, or add):

   proud   compelled to
                                      explain, justify
   embarrassed
                                      eager to talk about it
   guilty
                                      nothing in particular

   _____

6. To minimize the hard feelings between students in my class and their friends, (or between my class and other classes), I try to . . .

7. I think gifted students are like . . . (Please describe them. You may wish to do this by making two columns: in one, list all the ways in which gifted kids are similar to other children at a particular age level. In the other, list all the ways in which the gifted kids seem different from other students their age.)

8. What do I expect of my gifted students as a group and individually?

9. The gifted kids I have the EASIEST time with are those that are:
   _____
   or do: _____
   or are good in: _____

10. The gifted kids I have the HARDEST time with are those that are:
    or do: _____
    or are good in: _____

11. When I can't answer a student's question, or feel that "I'm losing control" of the class, I do these things: _____

12. The best thing(s) I have to offer my gifted students is (are) my: __

13. I think I could improve my teaching by . . .

14. I think as an education community, we need to change or improve gifted ed programs in the following ways:

    a.

    b.

    c.

    d.

15. I'm involved with the following activities (check and rate in terms of time: 1 = devote major time to this; 2 = devote a fair amount of time to this; 3 = spend little time on this; blank = spend no time on this):

curriculum development	____	training others	____
prep time	____	counseling students	____
politicking	____	identifying students	____
parent communication	____	scheduling	____
staff communication	____	applying for grants	____
continuing ed for myself	____	piloting new techniques	____
preparing budgets	____	open houses / meetings	____

16. In terms of workload, my job is

    fairly demanding   enough to
    easy   drive one crazy

17. One thing I'd like to hear from other people (parents, administrators, colleagues) is:

18. One thing I'd like to change or do differently in the program is:

    There are, of course, no right answers to the questions above, "only six more questions."

Recommended Resources for Social and Emotional Growth

Alberti, Robert E. and Michael L. Emmons. *Your Perfect Right: A Guide to Assertive Living* (San Luis Obispo, CA: Impact Publishers, 1990).

Canfield, Jack and Harold C. Wells. *One Hundred Ways to Enhance Self-Concept in the Classroom* (Boston, MA: Allyn & Bacon, 1994).

Chase, Larry. *The Other Side of the Report Card: A How-To-Do-It Program for Affective Education, Grades 4–6* (Glenview, IL: Scott, Foresman & Company, 1975).

Houston, Jean. *The Possible Human—A Course in Extending Your Physical, Mental, and Creative Abilities* (Boston, MA: J.P. Tarcher, Inc., 1982).

Palmer, Patricia. *The Mouse, The Monster And Me—Assertiveness for Young People* (San Luis Obispo, CA: Impact Publishers, 1984).

Rainer, Tristine. *The New Diary—How to Use a Journal for Self-Guidance and Expanded Creativity* (Los Angeles, CA: J.P. Tarcher, Inc., 1979).

INDEX

155

Other Great Books from Free Spirit

Teaching Gifted Kids
in the Regular Classroom
Strategies and Techniques Every Teacher Can Use
to Meet the Academic Needs of the Gifted and Talented
by Susan Winebrenner
Field-tested, step-by-step techniques for teaching
gifted students without losing control, causing
resentment among other students, or spending
hours preparing extra materials.
For teachers, all grades.
$21.95; 168 pp.; softcover; 8½" x 11"

Teaching Young Gifted Children
in the Regular Classroom
Identifying, Nurturing, and Challenging Ages 4–9
*by Joan Franklin Smutny, M.A., Sally Yahnke Walker, Ph.D.,
and Elizabeth Meckstroth, M.Ed., M.S.W.*
This book provides proven, practical ways to recognize and nurture young gifted children and create a
learning environment that supports *all* students.
For teachers, preschool through grade 4.
$29.95; 240 pp.; softcover; 8½" x 11"

The Kid's Guide to Social Action
How to Solve the Social Problems You Choose—
and Turn Creative Thinking into Positive Action
Revised, Expanded, and Updated Edition
by Barbara A. Lewis
Newly revised, expanded, and updated, this award-
winning guide includes everything kids need to make
a difference in the world, from inspiring true stories
to reproducible forms and up-to-date resources.
For ages 10 & up.
$16.95; 232 pp.; softcover; B&W photos and illus.; 8½" x 11"

Other Great Books from Free Spirit

The Gifted Kids' Survival Guide
A Teen Handbook
Revised, Expanded, and Updated Edition
by Judy Galbraith, M.A., and Jim Delisle, Ph.D.
Revised, expanded, and updated, this book features
new facts, findings, and insights about giftedness,
school survival, goal-setting, expectations, relationships, mental health issues, and much more.
For ages 11–18.
$14.95; 304 pp.; softcover; illus.; 7¼" x 9¼"

The Gifted Kids' Survival Guide
For Ages 10 and Under
Revised and Updated Edition
by Judy Galbraith, M.A.
First published in 1984, newly revised and updated,
this book has helped countless young gifted children
realize they're not alone, they're not "weird," and
being smart, talented, and creative is a bonus, not a
burden. Includes advice from hundreds of gifted kids.
For ages 10 & under.
$9.95; 88 pp.; softcover; illus.; 6" x 9"

The Survival Guide for Parents of Gifted Kids
How to Understand, Live With, and Stick Up
for Your Gifted Child
by Sally Yahnke Walker
Up-to-date information about giftedness, gifted
education, problems, personality traits, and more,
written by an educator of gifted kids and their parents.
For parents of children ages 5 & up.
$10.95; 152 pp.; softcover; illus.; 6" x 9"

Other Great Books from Free Spirit

Stick Up for Yourself!
Every Kid's Guide to Personal Power and Positive Self-Esteem
by Gershen Kaufman, Ph.D., and Lev Raphael, Ph.D.
Simple text teaches assertiveness, responsibility, relationship skills, choice making, problem solving, and goal setting. Kids learn to grow a "feelings vocabulary" and "store" happiness and pride.
For ages 8–12.
$9.95; 96 pp.; softcover; illus.; 6" x 9"

A Teacher's Guide to Stick Up for Yourself
A 10-Part Course in Self-Esteem and Assertiveness for Kids
by Gerri Johnson, Gershen Kaufman, Ph.D., and Lev Raphael, Ph.D.
Includes 14 reproducible handout masters.
For teachers, grades 3–7.
$18.95; 128 pp.; softcover; 8½" x 11"

Perfectionism
What's Bad About Being Too Good?
by Miriam Adderholdt-Elliot, Ph.D.
Explores the differences between healthy ambition and unhealthy perfectionism, explains why some people become perfectionists, and gives strategies for getting out of the perfectionist trap.
For ages 13 & up.
$9.95; 136 pp.; softcover; illus.; 6" x 9"

To place an order or to request a free catalog of SELF–HELP FOR KIDS®
materials, please write, call, email, or visit our Web site:

Free Spirit Publishing Inc.
400 First Avenue North • Suite 616 • Minneapolis, MN 55401-1724
toll-free 800.735.7323 • local 612.338.2068 • fax 612.337.5050
help4kids@freespirit.com • www.freespirit.com